DICKSON'S
JOKE TREASURY

Books by Paul Dickson

Think Tanks

The Great American Ice Cream Book

The Future of the Workplace

The Electronic Battlefield

The Mature Person's Guide to Kites, Yo-Yos, Frisbees, and Other Childlike Diversions

Out of This World: American Space Photography

The Future File

Chow: A Cook's Tour of Military Food

The Official Rules

The Official Explanations

Toasts

Names

There Are Alligators in Our Sewers & Other American Credos
by Paul Dickson and Joseph C. Goulden

On Our Own: A Declaration of Independence for the Self-Employed

Family Words

The Library in America

The New Official Rules

The Dickson Baseball Dictionary

Slang!

What Do You Call a Person From?

Timelines

Baseball's Greatest Quotations

On This Spot
with Douglas E. Evelyn

Dickson's Word Treasury: A Connoisseur's Collection of Old and New, Weird and Wonderful, Useful and Outlandish Words

DICKSON'S JOKE TREASURY

An Anthology of Gags, Bits, Puns, and Jests— And How to Tell Them

Paul Dickson

Illustrated by Don Addis

John Wiley & Sons, Inc.

New York ♦ Chichester ♦ Brisbane ♦ Toronto ♦ Singapore

Published by John Wiley & Sons, Inc.
All rights reserved. Published simultaneously in Canada.

Grateful acknowledgment is made for permission to reprint excerpts from the following:

Glenn Collins collection of *Chattanooga Choo Choo* jokes. Copyright © 1975 by The New York Times Company.

Kansas City tourist tips by William Tammeus from "Howdy Friend," *Kansas City Star-Times.*

"Do Its" from *Maledicta, the International Journal of Verbal Aggression,* Volume 4, edited by Reinhold Aman.

Cartoon by Don Addis on page 23 appears with the permission of *The St. Petersburg Times.*

Portions of the chapter "How to Tell a Joke" originally appeared in *Creative Living* magazine.

Library of Congress Cataloging in Publication Data:

Dickson, Paul.
 Dickson's joke treasury : an anthology of gags, bits, puns, and jests and how to tell them / Paul Dickson.
  p.   cm.
 ISBN 0-471-55666-1 (pbk.)
 1. American wit and humor. I. Title
PN6162.D46 1992
818'.540208—dc20   91-42415

Printed in the United States of America
10 9 8 7 6 5 4 3 2 1

*With special recognition of
the late Irving Hale and the late Russ Dunn, Sr.,
this book is dedicated
to the scores of joke tellers and hoarders
who let me borrow their best stuff.
This legion of helpers know who they are,
but in case any of them try to squirm out of it,
they are all listed at the back of the book.
The author, of course, takes responsibility
for all the good jokes while the clunkers
should be blamed on those caring souls who
so generously helped.*

Preface

The main obligation is to amuse yourself.

—S. J. Perelman

I have always believed that one of the goals of a civilized life is putting together one's own joke collection. It is one of those few things one can do that requires no justification or mindless blather about relevance. It is in the same class as whipping up the perfect omelette or hitting a home run in that anyone who questions the importance of such deeds is *ipso facto* irrelevant and out of touch with mortal realities. Despite years of trial and error, I am still a flop as an omelette cook and, middle-aged fantasies notwithstanding, I've never hit a home run; but as for the joke book . . . my time has come.

In 1985 Leo Rosten made publishing history when he published his *Giant Book of Laughter* and made the following warranty to the reader:

If you do not receive an amplitude of pleasure from this book, do not hesitate to return it to me, with a check for the exact amount you paid. I will return your check within five days.

The same offer is hereby made for this book with the added sweetener that I will personally autograph each check and hand deposit it within *four* days.

PAUL DICKSON

Garrett Park, Maryland
June 1992

Contents

DICKSON'S
JOKE TREASURY

• INTRODUCTION •
Funny Formula Jokes

Men show their character in nothing more clearly than what they think laughable.

—Alexander Pope

"Why does a chicken cross the road?"
"That wasn't no chicken—that was my wife.

—Bennett Cerf

You don't have to be a psychologist to realize that the jokes a person dotes on are a direct reflection of the person who tells them. My fascination has always been for jokes with a comfortable and immediately recognizable format: formula jokes. These jokes start with a basic theme or formula and lend themselves to endless variation. Most of them are absurd to begin with and become more so as variation is piled on variation.

I believe that a fascination for this type of joke reveals the same kind of classical mentality that prefers sonnets over free verse, ballet over modern dance, and paper towels in public rest rooms over those damnable air blowers. If this also reveals a form of deep cultural conservatism, so be it.

Rather than getting bogged down in windy definitions, here are two admittedly subjective lists that quickly separate the joke universe into two major camps, which I have cleverly termed "formula" and "other."

A. Formula	**B. Other**
Gleefully corny	Sophisticated
Funny	Not so funny
Very short or very long	Longish
Akin to early Woody Allen movies	Akin to later Woody Allen films
Kids love 'em	Kids don't know what the hell you're talking about
Can be dirty	Can be sexually explicit
Geared to getting guffaws and groans	Pitched to polite laughter
Typical opening: "Two poodles go into a bar and order martinis. . . ."	*Typical opening:* "Two human beings go into a bar and order white wine. . . ."
The kind of joke you'd tell W. C. Fields, Fred Allen, or Joan Rivers	The kind of joke you'd tell Irving R. Levine, Dr. Joyce Brothers, or Ingmar Bergman
Told by people who worried that when the United States recognized Red China, Taiwan would get back at us by cutting off the supply of whoopie cushions	Told by people who fret about the incorrect use of the word "hopefully" and talk about dental flossing in public
Helps identify the teller as a person of grace, wit, and style	Does no such thing
Politically lost	Politically correct

◆ ◆ ◆

It is difficult to say exactly what goes into making a classic Column
A personality, but deep self-analysis has led me to believe that

in my own case, there were five very important incidents and influences. Here they are in chronological order presented for the insight and uplift of others.

I

My father loved the most basic joke and riddle forms. Although he could be quite serious, he was also the kind of man who thought, correctly, that his children should have full command of the basic formulaic questions and their rich array of answers. "What's black and white and red all over?" he would ask and then come up with one of a dozen variant answers. It was also his belief that no child should ever visit our house without being asked, "What's the difference between an elephant and a mailbox?" Intimidated, the kids would always say they didn't know, which gave him the chance to reply, "I'd never send you to mail a letter."

After years of training, one morning I approached my father with the variant question:

"Who was that ladle I saw you with last night?"

He thought for a minute and said he didn't know.

I beamed and shot back, "That was no ladle, that was a spoon."

Not to belabor the obvious, it was a proud moment for both of us.

II

I was born and brought up in Yonkers, New York, which ranks with Tickfaw, Louisiana, and Podunk, Massachusetts, as one of the most inherently funny names on the map of America. Unlike Tickfaw and Podunk, however, it also was loaded with funny people—Sid Caesar, Morey Amsterdam, and Art Carney all were born or lived there—and was, along with Hoboken, the place that comedians used as a place name for a gag and that songwriters used for tricky rhymes. ("We'll go to Yonkers, where true love conquers.") It rivaled Nantucket as a locale in limericks, and it is the only place in America from which letters to "Dear Abby" can be signed "Bonkers in Yonkers." Coming from Yonkers could not actually make one funnier or a better joke teller, but it certainly helped, and it certainly was not a handicap like coming from a euphoniously named place like Atlanta or Portland.

III

During the summers of 1959 and 1960, I worked for the Otis Elevator Company in Yonkers. I was in college, and each fall when I returned, my various professors would ask me what I had done during the summer. Almost without exception, a variation of the following exchange took place:

Prof: "What did you do last summer?"
Me: "I worked for an elevator company."
Prof: (Long pause) "I'll bet that had its ups and downs."

This was followed by studied professional laughter, which, as anyone who has come within five miles of an institution of high learning knows, is generally unlike any other sound on earth.

The first few times this ritual took place, I was vaguely irritated by these great teachers' smugness about a gag that had presumably been around since Elisha Graves Otis rigged his first elevator in New York City in 1852. Then it dawned on me that this gave these professors a great deal of pleasure, and I began to understand that one of the great gifts you can offer another person is a tidy straight line. During my second summer at Otis, I learned that other collegiate summer workers had participated in the same ritual.

Years later, the importance of the elevator joke was brought home to me when I ran into one of my old professors on the streets of New York. Did he recall the brilliant, if flawed, papers I had handed him? No. What he remembered was the fact that I had worked in an elevator factory, and he then repeated *his* joke.

Over the years, I've spoken with elevator operators and found that they are not only plagued with the ups-and-downs line, but also are hit with "I'm sure you raised a number of fine families in your time" and "Could you let me off on five if that's not taking you out of the way?" During a brief, ill-considered time in which I worked for a brokerage house, I discovered a group who were unable to say "Otis Elevator" without saying, "I wish I'd gotten in on the ground floor with that one."

IV

One night in 1963, while serving in the U.S. Navy, I consumed most of a bowl of highly seasoned soup. The man sitting next to me suddenly made a horrible noise, spat out the soup, and then bellowed, "This soup is full of flies." They were aphids, actually (or, as some people call them, plant lice), and were small enough to masquerade as large chunks of ground pepper in the dried mix from which the soup had been prepared.

Ever since then, I have experienced a slight wave of nausea upon hearing jokes that begin with the line, "Waiter, there's a fly in my soup!" Curiously, however, I have chosen to deal with my aphid trauma by putting together and including in this book what I think may be *the* definitive collection of such jokes—an effort akin to getting back on a horse after you've been thrown.

V

Finally, for reasons unclear, I enjoy a strange affliction that visits me in times of stress: When the going gets tough, my mind fills with a collection of quick, corny jokes that relate to the situation at hand. One example will suffice.

Whenever I have a physical exam and am about to suffer the particular probing that David Brenner calls the one that makes a person feel like a hand puppet, my mind fills with jokes. Once it was a series of convoluted puns ("No, thanks," she said, "I gave at the orifice"); another time it was limericks ("There once was a nearsighted proctologist . . ."). But the last time it was "Doc . . . Next" jokes. "Doc . . . Next" jokes? Glad you asked:

"Doc, I get this terrible pain in my back every time I bend over."
    "Then don't bend over. Next!"

"Doc, nobody ever pays any attention to me."
    "Next!"

☞

Given that I am a confirmed Column-A personality, it was only natural that when it came time for me to assemble my kind of jokebook it would dwell on those things I loved most: Little Willie rhymes, shaggy dogs, light bulb jokes, pearly gates stories, elephants, and many more of the great themes and formats.

After years of thinking about it, what prompted me to do it right was my growing realization that jokes need protection just as a fine old building might require protection from the wrecker's ball. The threat being posed is the creeping Column-B solemnization and academization of American humor. This came to my attention a few years back when I got on some master mailing list that brought me countless announcements for seminars and conferences on humor. I began reading papers and journal articles and even attended an international conference on the subject. The conclusion I reached was inescapable: Humor in general and jokes in particular are becoming something to be probed and fretted over like some skin disease.

Sparing many of the more horrible details, here is what I found:

• Jargon-laden reports on the psychological and physiological aspects of humor are being delivered and published with stunning regularity. They carry titles like "Interfacing Vicarious Superiority and Interactive Incongruity Humor Theories" and "The Psycho-Social Bases of Scatological Humor: The Intra-Psychic Conflict between Autonomy and Conflict." Having heard some of these topics presented, I can assure you that their titles are often their most mirthful and comprehensible element. No aspect of humor is safe from the academic dragnet as jokes and wisecracks are coded and crammed into computers to help people get ready for humor conferences now being planned into the next century. One group has already picked the topics for its 1994 and 1995 conferences, which are, respectively, "Epiphany: The Humor of Sudden Insight," and "Shibboleths: Humor for In-bonding and Out-bonding." Commenting on the phenomenon in the *New York Times* way back in 1973, Israel Shenker noted that things had already gotten to the point where "Tickling has generated a ponderous literature all its own. . . ."

• Human subjects have been hooked to electrodes, injected with chlorpromazine, given structured "wit tally" tests, and even had their blood drawn and analyzed in the name of solving the "humor problem." In academic circles, the word *problem* has been welded to the word *humor*, whether in a paper like "The Problem of Humor in the Icelandic Family Sagas" (delivered at the Third International Conference on Humor in 1982) or in an assertion like "the shaggy dog story suggests many problems for folklorists" (made in the *Journal of American Folklore*).

• Some of the results of this research are astonishing. Jokes, for instance, have been turned into the most objectionable symbols among the post-Freudian psychologists and folkloric analysts. Elephant jokes have been tagged a possible subterfuge for white hostility and aggression against blacks (*Psychoanalytic Re-*

view), and light bulb jokes are seen as symbols of our sexual and political impotence (*Journal of American Folklore*). To read about jokes in the land that begat Dorothy Parker, Fred Allen, and Harry Hershfield is to read about neurosis, guilt, and despair.

• Meanwhile, others are belaboring the most obvious points. One Ph.D., who obviously never heard a salesperson use a few jokes to warm up a prospect, has discovered that jokes are sometimes used to influence the behavior of others. Another breathlessly reveals that a sense of humor and intelligence are not always linked in humans. We are shown charts proving that jokes popular in Pakistan are not quite as funny when retold on the streets of Toronto and are presented with data showing us that fat women in jokes get more laughs than fat men, but that jokes about male absentminded professors go over better than jokes about their female counterparts. Others attend conferences to argue the extent to which jokes represent aggression and hostility and to what degree they are healthy. Still others debate the question of whether laughter represents pleasure or displeasure—yet nobody seems willing to grapple with Robert Benchley's position, taken in response to the humor scholarship of his time, that laughter represents suppressed sneezing.

• Finally, there is a growing utilitarian movement in humor, which has been sparked by such diverse items as a recent U.S. Air Force study determining that humor is good for military teamwork and the late Norman Cousins's over-reported therapy through laughter. Increasingly, humor is being seen as a powerful tool for enhancing self-esteem, feedback, leadership, teamwork, caring, sharing, tension management, communication, and all the other late-twentieth-century talk-show verities.

A more recent benefit to be claimed appeared in an article on laughter that appeared in the *Washington Post* on May 23, 1991. The key sentence read: "The exercise value of laughter is so great that William Fry, a psychiatrist at Stanford University School of Medicine, claims that laughing 100 times a day is the equivalent of 10 minutes of strenuous rowing."

These "discoveries" are often revealed by people who act as if all of this were unknown to Will Rogers, Jonathan Winters, James Thurber, George Ade, and several million others who operated in the dark ages before electronic biofeedback equipment and public discussion of the need for a high-fiber diet.

There is, of course, nothing wrong with this, save for the fact that the solemnity gets us away from the humor—the jokes, laughs, squirt flowers, and rubber noses. "Humor," E. B. White once wrote, "can be dissected, as a frog can, but the thing dies in the process and the innards are discouraging to any but the pure scientific mind." What follows amounts to a great army of live frogs that have been trained to attack if you even think about dissection. With any luck, you may experience what an early humor researcher described as ". . . clonic spasms of the diaphragm in numbers ordinarily about 18 . . . while the skin at the outer canthi of the eyes is characteristically puckered . . . a marked proper flexion of the trunk for its relief . . . the eyes often slightly bulge forwards and the lachrymal gland becomes active."

Enough. On to the jokes. Oh, yes, one final thing. This book comes with operating instructions, which are tucked into the back of the book in Chapter 28, "How to Tell a Joke."

· 1 ·

Flies in the Soup

This important formula joke, which dates back at least to the early days of vaudeville, has inspired the following accolade from British humorist Michael Watts, which appeared in his wonderfully corny book, *I say, I say!* "The diner who bawls 'Waiter, there's a fly in my soup!' is meat and drink to the Corny Jokester. He is the gagman's copy-book feed. 'Waiter, there's a fly in my soup!' surpasses, in my opinion, 'Why did the chicken cross the road?', 'Who was that lady I saw you with last night?' and all the rest, as the most prolific straight line in the history of Corn."

Watts paid further homage to the formula by listing 16 replies. Not bad, but here are 45 pure examples and 69 variations, including a few stolen from Watts.

"Hey, waiter, there's a fly in my soup!"
"Shhhhhh! Everyone will want one."

FLIES IN THE SOUP

"Waiter, there's a fly in my soup!"
"Don't apologize to me."

"Waiter, there's a fly in my soup!"
"Half a fly would be worse."

"Waiter, there's a fly in my soup!"
"At our restaurant, we guarantee you don't find a single fly."
"Whaddya mean?"
"Because they're all married."

"Waiter, there's a fly in my soup!"
"That's all right, sir. No extra charge."

"Waiter, there's a fly in my soup!"
"It can't be, sir, you're eating noon lunch—and this is a fly-by-night place."

"Waiter, there's a fly in my soup!"
"That's all right. It's not hot enough to burn him."

"Waiter, there's a fly in my soup!"
"Wring him out before you throw him away."

"Waiter, there's a fly in my soup!"
"Yes, sir—better sip it with care."

"Waiter, there's a fly in my soup!"
"So what! There's soup on your fly."
Or:
"Sir, you're fortunate there's no soup on your fly."

"Waiter, there's a fly in my soup!"
"Okay, I'll bring you a fork."

"Waiter, there's a fly in my soup!"
"I'm not the waiter, I'm the manager."

"Waiter, there's a fly in my soup!"
  "Force of habit, sir, the chef used to be a tailor."

"Waiter, there's a fly in my soup!"
  "Serves the chef right. I told him not to strain the broth through the fly swatter.

"Waiter, there's a fly in my soup!"
  "That's funny, there were two of them when I left the kitchen."

"Waiter, there's a fly in my soup!"
  "There's a fly that knows good soup."

"Waiter, there's a fly in my soup!"
  "No, sir, that is an essential bee vitamin."

"Waiter, there's a fly in my soup!"
  "Go ahead and eat him, there's more where he came from."

"Waiter, there's a fly in my soup!"
  "Oh, hell! I've mixed my orders again."

"Waiter, there's a F-L-Y in my alphabet soup."

"Waiter, there's a fly in my soup!"
  "Don't worry, sir—he's a good swimmer."

"Waiter, there's a fly in my soup!"
  "Funny—it's supposed to be mock-turtle."

"Waiter, there's a fly in my soup!"
  "Don't worry, sir—he's only showing off."

"Waiter, there's a fly in my soup!"
  "Nonsense, sir—we don't serve meat on Fridays."

FLIES IN THE SOUP

"Waiter, there's a fly in my soup!"
"That's not a fly, sir, it's just dirt in the shape of a fly."

"Waiter, there's a fly in my soup!"
"Just a moment, sir—I'll fetch a spider."

"Waiter, there's a fly in my soup!"
"I know, watch him dive for the parsley."

"Waiter, there's a fly in my soup!"
"Well, do you blame him?"

"Waiter, there's a fly in my soup!"
"Okay, here's a fly swatter."

"Waiter, there's a fly in my soup!"
"That's not a fly, that's raisin delight."

"Waiter, there's a fly in my soup!"
"What do you expect with the blue plate? A hummingbird?"

"Waiter, there's a fly in my soup!"
"What did you expect for seventy-five cents, a Cornish game hen?"

"Waiter, there's a fly in my soup!"
"Does that mean you'll be wanting dinner for two?"

"Herr ober! In miner suppe ist eine fliege!"
"Nicht mehr lange, mein heir, sehn sie die spinne am teller-and."

(Translation: "Waiter, there's a fly in my soup!"
"Not for long, sir. See that spider on the edge of the plate?")

"Waiter, there's a fly in my soup!"
"Sorry, I guess we forgot to put it on the menu."

"Waiter, there's a fly in my soup!"
   "Don't worry, the frog should snap it up any second now."

"Waiter, there's a fly in my soup!"
   "I know. It gives you a nice buzz, doesn't it?"

"Waiter, there's a fly in my soup!"
   "I'd like a second opinion."
"It's also too salty."

"Waiter, there's a fly in my soup!"
   "Big deal! So you can identify aircraft."

"Waiter, there's a fly in my soup!"
   "Just wait until you see the main course."

"Waiter, there's a fly in my soup!"
   "That's strange. What kind of soup is it?"

"Waiter, there's a fly in my soup!"
   "Ah, we've cornered him at last."

"Waiter, there's a fly in my soup!"
   "Oh, don't mind him; he's just washing his tennis sneakers."

"Waiter, there's a fly in my soup!"
   "If you wanted him with dessert, why didn't you say so?"

"Knock, Knock."
   "Who's there?"
   "Jupiter."
   "Jupiter who?"
   "Jupiter fly in my soup?"

"Waiter, there's a dead fly swimming in my soup!"
   "Nonsense, sir—dead flies can't swim."

FLIES IN THE SOUP

"Waiter, there's a fly swimming in my soup. What's he doing there?"

"Dunno, sir—looks like the breaststroke."

"Waiter, there's a fly swimming in my soup!"

"You're lucky, sir—there's usually only enough for them to wade in."

"Waiter, there's a fly in the bottom of my soup bowl! What does this mean?"

"Listen, Bud, if you want your fortune told, go see a gypsy."

Frog: "Waiter, there's no fly in my soup!"

"Waiter, what's that fly doing in this creamed soup?"

"Trying to improve her complexion."

"Waiter, there's a spider in my soup!"

"I'm sorry, sir, we must be out of flies."

"Waiter, there's a dead fly in my soup!"

"I'm sorry, sir, I'm sure he was alive when he left the kitchen."

"Hey, waiter, what's this dead fly doing in my soup?"

"It's the boiling water that kills them, sir."

"Waiter, there's a fly in my applesauce!"

"Of course, sir, it's a fruit fly."

"Waiter, there's a medfly in my soup!"

"I'm sorry, sir, it should have been in your salad."

"Waiter, what is this fly doing in my alphabet soup?"

"Learning to read?"

"Waiter, there's a fly in my moo shu pork!"

"That's nothing. Wait until you open your fortune cookie."

"Waiter, there are pennies in my soup!"

"Well, sir, you said you'd stop eating here if there wasn't some change in the food."

"Waiter, there's a fly in my ice cream!"

"Serves him right; let him freeze to death."

"Waitress, there's a fly in my soup!"

"I think you want the waiter. I'm here for another joke."

*   *   *   *

"Waitress, do you have frog's legs?"

"No, I just broke the heel off my shoe."

"Waiter, there's a hair in my soup!"

"Is it blond, sir? We're missing a waitress."

"Waiter, do you have frog's legs?"

"Certainly, sir."

"Good. Hop into the kitchen and bring me a hamburger."

"Waiter, I must say that I don't like all the flies in this dining room!"

"Tell me which ones you don't like and I'll chase them out for you."

"Waiter, what's that in my soup?"

"I'd better call the manager, sir, I can't tell one insect from another."

"Waiter, there's a hair in my apple pie!"

"I can't understand it, sir. Those apples were Baldwins."

"Waiter, I don't like the looks of this trout!"

"If it's looks you're after, why didn't you order goldfish?"

FLIES IN THE SOUP

"Hey, waiter, you've got your thumb in my bowl of soup!"
"Don't worry, sir, the soup isn't hot."

"Waiter!"
"Yes, sir, what can I do for you?"
"Waiter, I can't eat this stuff. Call the manager!"
"It's no use. He won't eat it, either."

"Waiter, you advertise blended coffee here, but this stuff is terrible."
"It is blended. It's a blend of yesterday's and today's."

"Waiter, you scratched the side of your nose with my spoon!"
"I'm sorry. Should I have used a fork instead?"

"Waiter, there's a caboose in my soup!"
"Yes, sir, this is a training table."

"Waiter, couldn't you make this corned beef lean?"
"Which way?"

"Waiter, take this steak back to the kitchen and tell the chef to chew it and choke!"
"I'm sorry sir, I can't. There are four cutlets, two chops, and a hamburger ahead of you."

"Waiter, will those waffles be long?"
"No, round."

"Waiter, this food isn't fit for a pig!"
"All right, I'll get you some that is."

"Waiter, there's an ax in my soup!"
"Naturally, sir, it's split pea."

"Waiter, I'd like a bowl of chili and a few kind words."
    "Here's the chili."
"How about the kind words?"
    "Don't eat the chili."

"Waiter, how much longer do I have to keep on waiting!"
    "I'm waiting, you're just sitting there."

"Waiter, this chicken is as tough as a paving stone."
    "That's because it's a 'Plymouth Rock,' sir."

"Waiter, what's the difference between the blue-plate and the white-plate specials?"
    "The white plate is fifty cents more."
"So the food is better?"
    "No, but we have to wash the plate."

"Waiter, how are your tongue sandwiches?"
    "They speak for themselves."

"Waiter, what happened to this lobster's other claw?"
    "He lost it in a fight."
"Well, bring me the winner."

"Waiter, how do you serve shrimps here?"
    "We bend down."

"Waiter, I'll have the spaghetti. Will it be long?"
    "I don't know; we never measure it."

"Waiter, this plate is wet!"
    "That's your soup, sir."

"Waiter, this sausage has meat at one end and bread at the other."
    "Well, sir, you know how hard it is to make both ends meet these days."

"Waiter, this soup tastes like turpentine!"
"It must be tea if it tastes like turpentine, because the soup tastes like kerosene."

"Waiter, I don't like this cheese!"
"But it's Gruyère, sir."
"Well, bring me some that grew elsewhere."

"Waiter."
"Yes, sir."
"What's this?"
"It's your soup, sir."
"Yes, but what kind?"
"It's bean soup, sir."
"I'm not asking what it has been, I'm asking what it is now."

"Waiter, this soup is spoiled!"
"Who told you?"
"A little swallow."

"Waiter, are there any eggs on your menu?"
"No, I wiped them off."

"Waiter, I'm so hungry I could eat a horse!"
"You certainly came to the right place."

"Waiter, I found a fly in the raisin bread!"
"Okay, okay, I'll trade you for a raisin."

"Waiter, bring me some tomatoes."
"Stewed, sir?"
"None of your damn business."

"Waiter, does the chef have pig's feet?"
"I can't tell, he's got his shoes on."

"Waiter, what's this terrible tough stuff?"
  "Sir, that's fillet of sole."
"Go back and get me a nice tender piece from the top half of the shoe."

"Waiter, there's no chicken in my chicken soup."
  "There's no horse in the horseradish, either."

"Waiter, this food gives me heartburn!"
  "What did you expect in a restaurant, sunburn?"

"Waiter, there's a button in my soup!"
  "Typographical error, sir, it should be mutton."

"Waiter, isn't this toast burnt?"
  "No, sir, it just fell on the floor."

"Waiter, bring me some tomato juice for a pickup."
  "Yes, sir, and what will you have for yourself?"

"Waiter, there's a hair in my soup!"
  "Quite natural, sir, it's rabbit soup."

"Waiter, these eggs should be turned over."
  "Turned over?"
"Turned over to the Museum of Natural History."

"Waiter, what's this fly doing in my soup?"
  "About ten miles an hour."

"Waiter, do you serve crabs here?"
  "We serve anyone; sit down."

"Waiter, there's a fly bothering me!"
  "Shall I call a policeman, sir?"

"Waiter, there's a dead fly in my soup!"
  "What do you want us to do, sir, have a funeral?"

FLIES IN THE SOUP

"Waiter, just look at this chicken; it's nothing but skin and bones!"
  "All right, sir, I'll go get the feathers."

"Waiter, look at the chicken you just served me. One leg is shorter than the other."
  "Are you planning to eat it, sir, or dance with it?"

"Waiter, do you have eczema?" asked the patron, noticing the waiter scratching his face.
  "No, sir, just what's on the menu."

Waiter: "Can I help you with your soup, sir?"
Diner: "Help me? What do you mean?"
Waiter: "Well, sir, from the sound, I thought you might wish me to drag you ashore."

"Flier, there's a weight in my soup."

· 2 ·

At the Pearly Gates

As formula jokes go, it is one of our oldest. Early examples remind us of grimmer times:

St. Peter: "Young man, how did you get here so quickly?"
Young man: "Flu."

In fact, it is hard to find a joke book from any period or on any topic that does not have at least one pearly gates joke. For instance, here is one from a 1915 automotive joke book titled *Funabout Fords:*

St. Peter stood at the pearly gates and examined those who would enter. One of the questions he seemed to think important related to automobiles.

"What kind of car did you own?" he asked a large, portly soul.
"A Packard," replied the l.p.s.

"I am sorry," said St. Peter, "but that does not help you. You will have to go down."

"Did you have an auto?" he asked a long, lean bean.

"I did, sir—a Pierce-Arrow."

"Too bad," said St. Peter. "Please press the lower button."

"And you, little man, did you own a machine?"

"Yes, sir, I did," replied a spry little fellow, starting to enter the elevator.

"What was it?"

"A Ford," replied the s.l.f.

"Come in," said St. Peter, throwing open the gates. "You've had your hell on earth."

A *New York Times* article from June 7, 1991, on the festival of St. Yves (a saintly lawyer from Nantes and the patron saint of lawyers) held in Treguier, France, suggests that the formula could be six centuries old. To quote the *Times*: "A popular Breton legend has it that when Yves died he accompanied a group of deceased nuns to St. Peter's Gate. When the nuns asked to enter St. Peter told them that Heaven already had plenty of nuns, so they would have to wait in Purgatory. Then Yves asked to enter, and St. Peter said: 'You can enter immediately: We don't yet have a single lawyer.'"

Starting with the next joke, which appears to be the grandaddy of all American pearly gates stories, here is a roughly chronological collection of them leading up to some very recent examples.

A noted member of the clergy approaches the pearly gates and is told that there is no room in heaven. He will have to wait for some years while new accommodations are built.

He puts up a fuss and St. Peter finally tells him that he will let him in on one provision: that he help solve a major mystery.

It seems that with millions crowded into heaven, Adam and Eve, who were among the leading celebrities, have been lost.

The minister says, "I'll be back in a few minutes."

St. Peter is stunned when the minister arrives a few minutes later with a man and woman in tow.

"How were you able to find them?" says St. Peter.

"Simple! I just looked for a couple without navels."

"You're not due for another ten years," says St. Peter to the new arrival. "Who's your doctor?"

Most salesmen get in heaven,
In spite of how they rate—
Before St. Peter spots them,
A foot's inside the gate.

Woman: "I have come to join my husband."

St. Peter: "What was his name?"

Woman: "William Smith."

St. Peter: "That's hardly enough for me to identify him, as we have many William Smiths here. Can you tell me anything else about him?"

Woman: "Well, just before he died, he said that if I ever slept with another man, he'd turn over in his grave."

St. Peter: "Oh, you mean Whirling Willie."

The dead waiter's wife, after numerous attempts, contacts him through a medium.

"Sam, Sam, I can't believe it's really you," she says joyfully. "Speak to me."

A faint voice is heard: "I can't—it's not my table."

A stockbroker seeks admission to the pearly gates.

"Who are you?" says St. Peter.

"I am a Wall Street broker."

"What do you want?"

"I want to get in."

"What is it that entitles you to admission?"

"Well, for one thing, the other day I saw a decrepit old crone on Broadway and handed her a nickel."

"Is that in the records, Gabriel?"

"Yes, St. Peter."

"What else have you done?"

"Well, the other night I was crossing the Brooklyn Bridge, and I ran into a half-frozen newsboy and I gave him a nickel."

"Gabriel, is that on the records?"

"Yes, St. Peter."

"What else have you done?"

"That's all I can think of."

"What do you think we ought to do with this guy, Gabriel?"

"Give him back his dime and tell him to go to hell."

An ardent golfer dies and finds himself at the pearly gates. St. Peter tells the man he has lived an exemplary life and that he can go right in.

The man asks, "St. Peter, where is the golf course?"

"I'm terribly sorry," replies St. Peter, "but that's one thing we don't have here."

The man turns and allows that he will see if the situation is any better in hell.

On the road to hell, he is greeted by an imp who has already heard of the golfer's rejection of heaven.

"This way, sir," says the imp, "the finest tournament-quality 18 holes you are likely to find this side of Augusta, Georgia."

The golfer looks around and agrees that it is the finest course he has ever seen.

"Fine," he says to the imp. "Get me some sticks and balls and I'll have the game of my life."

"I'm sorry, sir, we don't have any."

"What?" says the man. "No balls or clubs for a fine course like this?"

"No, sir," says the imp fiendishly, "that's the hell of it."

A bishop and a congressman arrive at the pearly gates. St. Peter greets them and says that he is going to give them immediate room assignments.

"Bishop, here are the keys to one of our nicest efficiency units. And for you, Mr. Congressman, the keys to our finest penthouse suite."

"What?" says the bishop. "This is unfair."

"Listen," says St. Peter, "bishops are a dime a dozen up here, but this is the first congressman we've ever seen."

A woman goes to a medium in hopes of communicating with the spirit of her late husband, Sam. The medium goes into a deep trance, and after a while a voice says, "Emily, is that you?"

"Sam, I'd know your voice anywhere. How are you?"

"Fine."

"And how is it there—where you are?"

"Wonderful. Today the sky is deep blue, the temperature is perfect, and the grass is deep and high. And the cows are everywhere—beautiful cows of every color."

"Isn't that amazing," says Emily. "I had no idea there'd be cows in heaven."

"Heaven?" says Sam. "Who's talking about heaven? I'm a bull in Minnesota."

An oil company executive arrives at the pearly gates only to hear that the quota for oilmen has been met. St. Peter tells him, "The only possible way for you to enter is to somehow get one of the oilmen already here to leave."

The new arrival thinks for a while and then hits on the answer:

He will create the rumor that oil has been discovered in hell and see if it will cause one of the oilmen in heaven to go over to the other side. St. Peter thinks it will be a good test, and the rumor is planted.

Within a few hours, there is a stampede through the pearly gates, and all of the oilmen in heaven have bolted.

Suddenly an astonished St. Peter notices that the man who wanted to enter is starting to run in the direction of hell.

"Where are you going?" he calls.

Over his shoulder the man calls back, "Well there may be something to the report after all."

Three nuns perish in a bus wreck and shortly thereafter they all arrive at the pearly gates, where St. Peter greets them and says, "I'll ask each of you a question, and if you answer correctly, I'll let you into heaven."

The first nun steps up and St. Peter asks, "Who was the first man on earth?"

"That's easy," she says. "Adam."

The gates open and she is admitted.

The second nun is asked the name of the first woman; she answers Eve and is admitted.

The third nun steps up and St. Peter says, "What did the first woman say to the first man when she first saw him?"

The nun starts, looks around despairingly, rolls her eyes, wrings her hands, and says, "Gee, that's a hard one!"

The clouds part and the gates open.

A man comes home to his apartment one day to find evidence that his wife has just been engaged in an extramarital romp. In fact, the smell of the other man's cigar is still in the air.

Suddenly, he gets the idea of trying to catch the guy. He runs out on the apartment's balcony, sees the cigar-smoking man leaving, runs back into the apartment, grabs the refrigerator, runs to the balcony, and drops it on the man with the cigar. The man who dropped the refrigerator then has a heart attack and dies.

Moments later, three men approach the pearly gates. St. Peter begins by asking how each died.

"I was minding my own business when I was hit by a refrigerator," says the first man.

"I died from the exertion of lifting and carrying a refrigerator," says the second.

The third man steps forward and says, "I was hiding inside this refrigerator and . . ."

A nun, Sister Margaret, goes to heaven and finds that she must wait to gain admission.

St. Peter comes over and says to her, "Why don't you go back to earth and relax for a few weeks? Check in with me every week or so."

After a week, she calls and says, "St. Peter, this is Sister Margaret. Everything is going well except for the fact that I smoked a cigarette."

"I think we can overlook that. Call me back next week."

The following week she calls and says, "Peter, this is Margaret . . . I had a few drinks last night, hope you don't mind."

St. Peter replies, "I think we can forgive you a few drinks. Your accommodations should be ready in a week or so."

A week later, she calls again: "Pete, this is Meg. Forget it."

A pope dies, goes to heaven, and is greeted by St. Peter. St. Peter explains that all is equal in heaven—no preference is ever given because of one's earthly station. The pope says, "That's as it should be in heaven."

Later the pope is standing in the cafeteria line, and a man wearing a white jacket with a stethoscope sticking out of the pocket walks to the front of the line and takes a tray.

"Did you see that?" the pope says to St. Peter. "You told me everyone was equal here."

"Oh, don't mind him," replies St. Peter. "That's God—he likes to play doctor once in a while."

A senator dies and goes to heaven. Upon passing through the pearly gates, he notices one of his Senate colleagues in the company of a most beautiful woman.

"Senator," says the newcomer, "it is indeed a pleasure to see a member of the world's greatest deliberative body rewarded so justly."

"Reward, hell," says the old senator. "I'm her punishment."

St. Peter has had a rough day and it occurs to Jesus Christ that he could use a little time off.

"Go get a cup of coffee," he says. "I can handle the pearly gates while you're gone."

St. Peter takes him up on the offer, and Christ takes over. Nothing happens for the first few minutes, but then an old man comes shuffling up the path to heaven.

"What have you done to enter the kingdom of heaven?" he asks rather routinely.

"Not much," says the old man. "I am just a poor carpenter who has led a quiet life. The only remarkable thing about my life was my son."

"Your son?" Christ asks with obvious interest.

"Yes, he was quite a son. He went through a most unusual birth and later a great transformation. He also became known throughout the world and is still loved by many."

Christ looks at the man, embraces him tightly, and says, "Father, father!"

The old man hugs him back and asks, "Pinocchio?"

Three Jews arrive at the pearly gates, and St. Peter greets them by saying, "Fellows, we're running short on space so I'm going to ask you some questions—and just to make it tough, they will be about other religions. If you answer correctly, you get right in, but if you make a mistake, you will have to wait."

The first man is asked to tell the story of the life of Buddha.

"I won't even try," he says as he heads off toward the waiting area.

The same thing happens when the second man is asked to describe the life of Mohammed.

But when the third man is asked to tell the life of Jesus Christ, he tells the story in absolutely perfect detail from the moment of his birth to his crucifixion.

"That's absolutely remarkable," says St. Peter, adding, "There are very few priests who could tell it as well as you just did. But you're not done. Please, sir, what happened after the crucifixion?"

"Well, sir, he is buried in a cave, but on the morning of the third day the stone rolls away from the mouth of the cave. At this moment he rises out of the tomb, and if he sees his shadow, that means we will have six more weeks of winter."

Two priests are killed in an automobile accident. Upon arriving at the pearly gates, they are informed that the computer is down and that they will have to go back to earth for a week.

"Fellows," says St. Peter, "you can go back as anything you'd like and because the computer is down, nothing will count against you."

The first priest tells St. Peter that he had always dreamt of being an eagle, soaring over the Rocky Mountains.

"Go," says St. Peter. "You're an eagle."

The second priest first reconfirms that whatever he does will not go into his record, and then says, "Well, I've always wanted to be a stud."

"Go," says St. Peter. "You're a stud."

A week passes and the archangel Gabriel comes to St. Peter to say that the computer is back in operation, and it is now time for him to fetch the two priests.

"Well," says St. Peter, "the first guy will be easy to find. He's flying over the Rockies near the Colorado-Wyoming border. The other guy's going to be a lot harder to find: He's somewhere inside a snow tire in Minnesota."

The gate between heaven and hell breaks, and St. Peter calls over to the devil, "It's your turn to fix it."

"Sorry," says the devil. "We are too busy fixing our heating system to worry about a little thing like a gate."

"If you don't fix it," says St. Peter, "I'll have to sue you for breaking our working agreement."

"Is that so?" says the devil. "Where are you going to find a lawyer?"

St. Peter greets a lawyer at the pearly gates with unusual warmth.

"Gee," says the lawyer, "does everybody get this kind of treatment?"

"You're not just anyone," St. Peter replies. "We seldom get lawyers who are as distinguished and old as you."

"But I'm only 48," says the lawyer.

"Funny," says St. Peter. "You've billed for so many hours we thought you were 80."

Three men arrive at the gates of heaven at the same time. St. Peter tells them they all have been admitted, and he will assign each of them a vehicle to use during their eternal stay. He says that he will assign the vehicle based on their marital fidelity.

He asks the first man if he had been a faithful husband and is told that he never strayed from the bed of the woman he loved. St. Peter hands him the keys to a Rolls Royce.

HS, students favorite joke

The second man comes forward, admits to a few indescreet moments early in his marriage and is awarded the keys to a Plymouth.

The third man steps up and confesses, "Sir, I have been a bad husband who had countless extramarital affairs and brief sexual encounters. The only thing I can say in my defense is that I did love my wife."

St. Peter thinks for a moment and offers the man an old 10-speed bicycle.

A few days later, the man on the bike sees the man who won the Rolls with his car at the side of the road. The virtuous man is sprawled across the hood of his car crying uncontrollably.

"Pal, what's up? You shouldn't be crying. Here you are in heaven with the finest car ever built."

"I know, I know," sobbed the man with the Rolls, "but I just saw my wife and she was riding a skateboard."

Finally, this one, which is not a pearly gates story but is set in heaven:

Two fine and devout Irish ladies end up in heaven.

"Isn't this grand, Bridget? Every night we go to bingo, there's a lot of singing and dancing, and they have all the old Alan Ladd movies."

"Yes, indeed, Gertrude, and you know if it wasn't for that silly oat bran, we'd have been here ten years earlier."

·3·

The Lowest Form of the Lowest Form

If the pun is the lowest form of humor—also the lowest form of pastry—the lowest form of pun is the knock-knock joke. This is what makes knock-knocks so appealing. Among their remarkable qualities is their defiance of scholarly analysis. Those who try to analyze them are destined to bog down in mindless babble within a sentence or two. ("They are joking parables of comic tentativeness and psychological expansion," wrote one analyst, who obviously never said, "Disraeli who? Disraeli too much.")

The paradox ("Paradox who? Paradox better than one if you're really sick") is that while they defy intellectualizing, they are intellectually demanding. This very point was made by John F. Gilbey (the pseudonym of a closet knocker who has sworn me to secrecy), who wrote, "Some will snort at this, but what do they know? They are the same species who believe that chess is more cerebral than checkers. For them, solve this: Piranha . . . What'd I tell you. It's tough. But to veteran knockers used to cosmic cerebration it's no problem: 'Piranha old gray bonnet. . . .' " He adds, "Not only are knock-knocks intellectually based, they are also great nostalgia. I never hear Aardvark without thinking of Jolson (that's enough of a clue), or Agatha without thinking of Sinatra, or that thing as the string he had the world on, or Avon without recalling Garbo." Some of us are unable to hear the word "meritricious" without adding ". . . and a happy new year."

Gilbey also believes that knock-knocks have resisted the full press of a major fad because they are intellectually too demanding for most.

Knock-knocks are also the jocular vehicle for any name you can think of:

Knock, Knock.
  Who's there?
  Desdemona.
  Desdemona who?
  Desdemona Lisa still hang on the gallery wall?

No name is safe whether it be Anita Loos (Anita Loos some weight, that's what I need to lose), Don Ameche (I'll be Don Ameche in a taxi, Honey), or Will Durant (Will Durant be paid this month or not?). Disraeli? Disraeli too much. Once you start with these, it is hard to think about certain individuals without the proper ritualistic response knocking about in your head. Keir Dullea, for instance, is as important to knock-knocking as Nantucket is to limericks (Keir Dullea, gone tomorrow; On a Keir Dullea you can see forever, etc.).

They can also be topical:

Knock, Knock.
  Who's there?
  Sagittarius.
  Sagittarius who?
  Sagittarius State Baker.

Like the sonnet and Japanese haiku, the knock-knock format offers great freedom within a disciplined framework. Scholars study the jokes, kids trade them on playgrounds, and sophisticated people use them as a vehicle for the most convoluted punning.

What is more, the properly atrocious punning of the knock-knock is still with us and afflicting headline writers at some of our great newspapers and magazines. A 1984 Henry Mitchell column in the *Washington Post* on doomsday predictions was slugged "Armageddon Sick of All This Talk" (a perfect knock-knock tag), and almost everybody who has written about the new crop of Nordic tennis stars feels compelled to title their observations "The Swede Smell of Success" (a weak replay of the knock-knock that ends with "Ida, Swedish apple cider").

The knock-knock joke has not only surived, but has become international; it's liable to show up anywhere, including the London *Times Literary Supplement*, which recently contained this fine state-of-the-art example:

Knock, Knock.
    Who's there?
    Wystan.
    Wystan who?
Wystan civilization is indeed in trouble if in times of crisis it cannot produce anything profounder than the knock-knock joke.

The paradox (Paradox is better than no docs) is that the British seem to take the knock-knock more seriously than we do. When the Soviet submarines were showing up in Swedish waters in the mid-1980s, the London *Standard* ran a cartoon with a Swedish diver knocking on the conning tower of a Soviet sub:

Sven.

Sven who?

Sven are you going to come up and surrender?

Some are, in fact, uniquely suited to English accents (as well as a sense of the grotesque).

Knock, Knock.

Who's there?

Amsterdam.

Amsterdam who?

Amsterdam is like plum jam, but made from 'amsters.

(American version: Amsterdam tired of these knock-knock jokes I could scream.)

In fact, a British writer, Eric Korn, has come up with a major advance in the writing of knock-knock jokes. In the review of Gyles Brandreth's 1984 classic *1,000 Knock Knocks,* in the aforementioned *Times Literary Supplement,* Korn unveiled his scheme. What it lacks in clarity, it makes up for in derring-do and innovation:

> In this review I shall use the existential quantifier (x), which will here have the extended sense "there is (at least one) x such that x is knocking at the door and x is uttering the proposition 'my name is x' ". This, naturally, begs a number of questions: is the assertion true? is the "knocker's name" the knocker's name? is there a sense in which, etc., etc. For further discussion, see my forthcoming *The Ontological Knock; or Descartes est dehors, if not before dehors.* Meanwhile, the first four lines of any knock-knock joke may be represented by the lucid expression " (x);?"

Korn's discovery will not be used in the rest of this chapter—but it is a useful tool for those who collect knock-knocks and need to save space:

(Dolores);?
Delores be an England.

Knock-knocks are also extremely satisfying both in the reciting and, for those with the gift, in the creating. To create a really first-rate knock-knock is the mental equivalent of a golfer's hole-in-one. Sit back and listen to the testimonials:

J. C. Y., Sr., a lawyer from Williamsport, Pennsylvania, recalls:

In 1934 when I was 31 years old I was a delegate to the annual meeting of the American Bar Association in Milwaukee, Wisconsin. Knock-knock jokes were at their height. I had occasion to use the men's room at my hotel. Upon returning to the lobby I ran into a lawyer friend from Philadelphia. I don't know why but something I had just seen inspired me. I said, "Knock, knock." My friend replied, "Who's there?" I said, "Ranger," and he said, "Ranger who?" I said, "Ranger clothes before leaving the men's room."

It is hard to think of better testimonial to any form of humor than an 80-year-old man's ability to recall a joke he'd made up 49 years earlier; but others come close.

Mike Thaler, who has written a number of knock-knock jokes and is the reigning "Riddle King," says:

Kids just go crazy over them. You stand in front of a room full of them and say "Knock-knock" and you are almost knocked over by the roar of "Who's there?" You know the one that they love the most?

Knock, Knock.
　Who's there?
　Honda.
　Honda who?
　Your hondaware is showing.

Before moving on, it is only right that we introduce the knock-knock Thaler feels is his personal best:

Knock, Knock.
　Who's there?
　Energize.
　Energize who?
　Her hair is blond energize are blue.

If you look hard enough, other important bits of testimonial show up . . . and at the most opportune moments. On a Friday afternoon in September 1981, I was stuck in the airport in Hartford, Connecticut, waiting for a long-delayed plane. I began amusing myself by studying the local phone books, looking for new knock-knock ideas. Suddenly it hit me. Here I was—a man in my forties, in a suit, standing next to a phone booth trying to figure out whether the name Rocco Spanducci could be turned into a serviceable knock-knock joke.

The absurdity of it troubled me, and I walked away thinking of friends who were, at that very moment, healing the sick or defending the innocent. It became clear that a Nobel prize was forever outside my reach. Sitting dejectedly, I tried to think of something else and picked up a few loose pages from the previous day's *Hartford Courant.* I started reading an article on Roald Dahl by a local free-lancer named Susan Slavet, and there were the lines from Dahl that I have now committed to memory: "I'm sixty-five and really just an adolescent. When I meet other fellows my age I think, 'There but for the grace of God go I.' I adore knock-knock jokes." According to the article of September 17, 1981, Dahl's favorite:

Knock, Knock.
    Who's there?
    Humphrey.
    Humphrey who?
    Humphrey ever blowing bubbles.

Dahl added, "I love that one. No one can ever figure it out."
    To hell with the Nobel (Nobel's no blue chips), I reasoned, thinking of the prolonged adolescence of Roald Dahl.

    Roald Dahl
    Roald Dahl who?
    Roald Dahl the barrel. We'll have a barrel of fun.

The most important force in contemporary knockery is William Cole, the poet and anthologist, who has written several knock-knock books and has six more on their way. He reports (you heard it here first)". . . the beginnings of a NAUGHTY KNOCK KNOCK BOOK ("U Thant lay me if you don't pay me!" "Vonnegut into your pants tonight!") Like that."*

* Cole's book of naughty knock-knocks will doubtlessly open up a whole new front. One of the rare few examples I have heard comes from my good friend, writer Joseph C. Goulden:
    Knock, Knock.
        Who's there?
        Fornication.
        Fornication who?
        Fornication like this, you should wear black tie.

Cole has not only functioned as an important collector and promoter of the form, but has created some of the genre's modern classics. His favorite original:

Knock, Knock.
 Who's there?
 Amaryllis.
 Amaryllis who?
 Amaryllis state agent—wanna buy a house?

Not only did he pen the original, he even came up with his own variation:

Knock, Knock.
 Who's there?
 Amarillo.
 Amarillo who?
 Amarillo-fashioned cowboy.

It can be argued, however, that Cole's single greatest contribution has been uncovering a major historical item. Dorothy Parker may well have invented the knock-knock joke. Cole came on this while reading Edmund Wilson's *The Twenties,* and he then wrote an article that was published in the *New York Times* on October 20, 1982. With Cole's permission, here are the words which knocked the knock-knock world on its ear:

There's a passage—and this was in 1920, mind you—where Wilson is discussing (and generally dismissing) the Algonquin Round Table. He writes: "At one time their favorite game consisted of near-punning use of words. 'Have you heard Dotty's "Hiawatha"—"Hiawatha nice girl till I met you." ' Marc Connelly's 'Honduras': something about 'the big Honduras [endurance] contest.' Somebody else's Benchley: 'Benchley [eventually]? Why not now?' (This was an advertising slogan.)" A later entry in Wilson's diary discusses Miss Parker, giving a couple of really bad knock-knocks, and this rather good one:

Knock, Knock.
>Who's there?
>Scrantoknow.
>Scrantoknow who?
>Scrantoknow you're appreciated.

"Dorothy," Mr. Wilson says, "thought they were not right unless the word began the sentence. . . ."

Cole admits that they weren't actually called knock-knocks and argues that the key word must appear at the beginning of the punch line; but these are minor points. Before this, it had been assumed that the jokes were created by college students in the 1930s. It would now appear that the 1930s was the period in which they came into their own. During the early Depression years, the movement grew slowly.

Then, in the summer of 1936, they became what *The Literary Digest* termed America's "newest nonsense craze" with knock-knocks ringing "in everyone's ears." It hit first in the colleges in May and was carried forward by orchestra leader Vincent Lopez, who composed and recorded the song "Knock Knock Who's There," containing some of the most popular examples. He got no fewer than five thousand letters with knock-knocks he had left out. Hal Kemp also made a record of the Lopez song; Paramount made a short knock-knock comedy; and the Dell Publishing Company published the first knock-knock book.* Newspapers offered

---

* That book, Knock, Knock, by Bob Dunn, which originally cost a dime, has become one of the hardest-to-find items of knock-knock memorabilia. The Library of Congress doesn't even have a copy, nor does the San Francisco Public Library, which houses the nation's largest public collection of humor books.

cash prizes for the best knock-knocks, and any columnist worthy of the name found a way to work a few into his or her column. Heywood Broun made up this one:

> Knock, Knock.
> Who's there?
> A gang of vigilantes with machine guns, leather and brass knuckles to thump anybody who persists in playing this fool knock-knock game.

Before it was all over, CBS had banned the song from its live radio shows after a few suggestive puns had been worked into versions of the song, and Whitney Bolton, a columnist for the New York *Morning Telegraph*, had termed it "a mental disease."

For knock-knocks, there was never to be another 1936, but the form never went into eclipse, either. They became as much a ritual of childhood as marbles and hopscotch had been to earlier generations, and there were always adults who, as John Gilbey put it, couldn't hear the word *Avon* without thinking of Garbo (Avon to be alone) or hear *aardvark* without thinking of Al Jolson (Aardvark a million miles for one of her smiles . . .).

Today there are an astonishing number and variety of knock-knocks. One man, whom we will meet a bit later, has collected 131,000 of them, and they come in a number of variant forms, including:

The Novelty Knock-Knock
Knock, Knock.
> Who's there?
> It is I.
> Oh, a Harvard man.

THE LOWEST FORM OF THE LOWEST FORM

The Triple Comeback
Knock, Knock.
>Who's there?
>Eskimo, Christian, Italian.
>Eskimo, Christian, Italian who?
>Eskimo, Christian, Italian no lies.

The Shaggy Knock-Knock
>Will you remember me in five years?
>Yes.
>Will you remember me next year?
>Yes.
>Will you remember me next month?
>Yes.
>Will you remember me next week?
>Yes.
>Will you remember me tomorrow?
>Yes.
>Will you remember me in another minute?
>Yes.
>Will you remember me in another second?
>Yes.
>Knock, Knock.
>Who's there?
>You forgot me already?

The Special Occasion Knock
Knock, Knock.
>Who's there?
>Sensuous.
>Sensuous who?
>Sensuous such a nice person, I wish you a happy birthday.

The Celebrity Knock
Knock, Knock.
   Who's there?
   Baloney.
   Baloney who?
   Baloney God can make a tree.

This celebrity knock-knock was solicited from William Safire initially to test the premise that the busier and brighter the person, the more likely he is to have a fine knock-knock joke at the forefront of his brain. Safire's response proves this beyond a doubt.

The Series Knock-Knock
Knock, Knock.
   Who's there?
   Ether.
   Ether who?
   Ether bunny.

Knock, Knock.
   Who's there?
   Stella.
   Stella who?
   Stella nother Ether bunny.

Knock, Knock.
   Who's there?
   Samoa.
   Samoa who?
   Samoa Ether bunnies.

THE LOWEST FORM OF THE LOWEST FORM

Knock, Knock.
　Who's there?
　Consumption.
　Consumption who?
　Consumption be done about these Ether bunnies?

Scattered throughout this book are three collections of knock-knock jokes, each of which appears as a full-blown chapter (Chapters 10, 16, and 24). They have been seeded this way because their aforementioned intellectual richness would be too much to have all at once—the cerebral equivalent of three hot-fudge sundaes.

· 4 ·

"Doc . . . Next"

Imagine one of the Marx Brothers as your doctor and the scene is set for one of the simplest and eternally relevant formulas. A quick, healthy dose for this age of high-speed medicine:

"Doc, you're charging me ten dollars and all you did was paint my throat."

"What did you expect for ten dollars—wallpaper? Next."

"Doc, what should I do if my temperature goes up another point?"

"Sell! Next."

"Doc, how can I avoid falling hair?"

"Step to one side. Next."

"Doc, should I file my nails?"

"No. Throw them away like everybody else. Next."

"Doc, I just wanted to let you know that there is an invisible man in your waiting room."

"Tell him I can't see him now. Next."

"Doc, you've gotta do something for me. I snore so loudly that I wake myself up."

"In that case, sleep in another room. Next."

"Doc, my hair is coming out. What can you give me to keep it in?"

"A cigar box. Next."

"Doc, my child just swallowed a pen. What should I do?"

"Use a pencil. Next."

"Doc, my child just swallowed a dozen aspirins. What should I do?"

"Give him a headache. Next."

"Doc, is it a boy?"

"Well, the one in the middle is. Next."

"Doc, what am I really allergic to?"

"Paying my bills. Next."

"Doc, every bone in my body hurts."

"Be glad you're not a herring. Next."

"Doc, what would you take for this cold?"

"Make me an offer. Next."

"Doc, there's something wrong with my stomach."

"Keep your coat buttoned and nobody will notice it. Next."

"Doc, thank you so much for making this house call to see my husband."

"Think nothing of it. There is another man sick in the neighborhood, and I thought I could kill two birds with one stone. Next."

"Doc, there's a man outside with a wooden leg named Smith."

"What's the name of his other leg? Next."

"Doc, am I getting better?"

"I don't know—let me feel your purse. Next."

"Doc, am I going to die?"

"That's the last thing you're going to do. Next."

"Doc, how long will I live?"

"You should live to be 80."

"I am 80."

"What did I tell you? Next."

"Doc, this ointment you gave me makes my arm smart."

"Why not rub some on your head? Next."

"Doc, what should I do? I can't sleep at night."

"Sleep during the day. Next."

"Doc, what's the difference between an itch and an allergy?"

"About $25. Next."

"Doc, don't you think I should get a second opinion?"

"Sure. Come back tomorrow. Next."

"Doc, one night I dream I am in a wigwam, the next night I dream I am living in a teepee. What's happening to me?"

"Nothing. You're just too tents. Next."

"Doc, nobody can figure out what's wrong with me. I've got the oddest collection of symptoms."

"Have you had it before?"

"Yes."

"Well, you've got it again. Next."

"Doc, I think I've developed a split personality."

"Okay, go chase yourself. Next."

"Doc, what do you have for greying hair?"

"Nothing but the highest respect, sir. Next."

"Doc, I'm feeling a bit schizophrenic."

"That makes four of us. Next."

"Doc, what should I do about all these tiny little green men crawling all over my arms?"

"I don't know, but don't get any of them on me. Next."

"Doc, can you give me something for my head?"

"No thanks, I've already got one. Next."

"Doc, I think I've got a bad liver."

"Well, take it back to the butcher. Next."

"Doc, what's your best suggestion for this terrible halitosis [bad breath] of mine?"

"Lockjaw. Next."

"Doc, I have this terrible ringing in my ears."

"Don't answer. Next."

"Doc, I get this terrible pain in my back every time I bend over."

"Then don't bend over. Next."

"Doc, what should I take when I get run down?"

"The license number. Next."

"Doc, what do you charge for a visit?"

"$50 for the first visit and $25 for each visit thereafter."
"Well I'm here again."

"Fine, take the same thing as last time. Next."

"Doc, nobody ever listens to me."

"Next."

· 5 ·

Punintended

Obscene verse.

**—Alleged comment about a lewd poem,
Ben Johnson**

A man who could make so vile a pun would not scruple to pick a pocket.

—John Dennis

I never knew an enemy of puns who was not an ill-natured man. A pun is a noble thing per se; it fills the mind, it is as perfect as a sonnet. May my last breath be drawn through a pipe and exhaled in a pun.

—Charles Lamb

Punning is a talent which no man affects to despise but he that is without it.

—Jonathan Swift

. . . those most dislike puns who are least able to utter them.

—Edgar Allan Poe

A good pun may be admitted among the smaller excellencies of lively conversation.

—James Boswell

The pun is the lowest form of humor—when you didn't think of it first.

—Oscar Levant

F act. The world is divided into two kinds of people: those who love puns and those who don't. There is no middle ground.

Fact. One of the surest signs of crass insensitivity and general boorishness is a dislike of puns.

We not only repeat them, but tend to work them into conversation—spicing our humdrum world with word play. They are our gift. They can be gifts that keep on giving. For years I have been unable to look at a copy of *Natural History* magazine without recalling the title of an article on cannibalism: "One Man's Meat is Another Person."

Sadly, there are those who reject these gifts and frown in seafood restaurants where the restroom doors are marked "Gulls" and "Buoys," cringe in horror when the word tumescence is defined as a perfume for mummies, flee when they hear those wonderful words, "Knock, Knock," and wouldn't be caught dead in a place called the Dew Drop Inn.

56

A case in point. A few years ago, the *Washington Post* became a haven for headlines like the aforementioned "Armageddon Sick of All This Talk" (for a column on doomsday predictions), "Montgomery Council Ponders Cat Purrmits" (on a proposal to require cat licenses in Montgomery County, Maryland), "If You Knew Sushi" (for an article on the health risks of eating raw fish), and "Foxy Soviets Pelt the West" (for a story on fur exports from the Soviet Union). This fad was a boon for readers who like to start the day with coffee and puns and was not restricted to the *Post*. A commentator (average potato?) recently said that the *Los Angeles Times* ". . . has the highest incidence and best punning average of any major organ in the world." The fad is pretty much gone now, but a keen eye reveals an occasional gem that is still slipped in.

One of the reasons why the Golden Age of newspaper punning is over is that readers have written to these fine organs rejecting the notion that humor belongs in a newspaper. One such letter, published in 1975 in the *Washington Post*, said, "Can't something be done about the virulent pun disease that afflicts *The Post*?"

If punning is a disease, then it is a benign one that infects us when we are in the company of others or alone —in other words, when the throng is gone, the malady lingers on. "Even in solitude I think of queer verbal acrobatics," Louis Untermeyer once wrote, "There is the temptation to characterize a certain writer's heavy bandiage as elephantry . . . Trotzky's idea of teaching the young socialists how to shoot as a poor piece of Marxmanship . . . composers plagiarizing from Debussy as Debussybodies."

Serious punsters tend to dream of using a pun at exactly the right moment. Finding, for example, that a friend has fallen in love with the woman who attended him in the hospital so that we can allege that "he has taken a turn for the nurse," or running into an experimental psychologist and asking if "he is still pulling habits out of a rat."

This tendency to dream of puns was beautifully stated by Shirley Whittington in an article that first appeared in the *Toronto Globe and Mail* and that opened with these lines, "I dream of being asked to a dinner party where the hostess falls backward onto the table. 'Look out!' I shout. 'You'll burn your end at both candles.' Or I meet a sculptor in the street. 'Hi, you old chiseler,' I say. 'Still taking things for granite?'"

At sublime moments, these dreams come true as an event happens that is tailor made for a pun long stored in a deep fold of the brain. The pun has found its home and is blurted out at the perfect moment. In an ideal lifetime, this can be expected to happen only a half-dozen times, but to the true punster those moments are never forgotten.

Several years ago, I was sitting on the porch of a summer cottage with my brother-in-law. Two large pieces of earth moving equipment suddenly appeared on the dirt road in front of the cottage, and as they rumbled past my brother-in-law asked me what I thought was going on. I trembled with the monumental opportunity at hand and replied, "Simple. This has become a two backhoe road."

For me this was as gratifying as when a friend told me about a magazine she had started called *Woman's Work*. It had been put together on a shoestring, and she said that during the first months her creditors had been supportive and carried the fledgling magazine. Later that night, the pun came to me as I lay in bed, and first thing the next morning I called her to say, "I think that what you were trying to say last night is that *Woman's Work* is never dunned."

If we are really afflicted, we will manufacture a situation to fit a pun. A few summers back, a good friend bought an old and decrepit lantern at a flea market and got several of us to help him get it back into working order. I can't prove it, but I am almost positive he did this so that at the moment the lantern lit up he could say, as he did, "Aha! Many hands make light work."

♦ ♦ ♦

The following is a small collection of puns—some sophisticated, some infantile (the child, after all, is fodder to the man), and some worthy of the supreme accolade that can accrue to a pun: "atrocious."

♦ ♦ ♦

During a portion of Beethoven's Ninth in which there are no bass violin parts, one of the bassists passes a bottle of scotch around. The bass section becomes totally looped, but the conductor is unaware of what is going on. His assistant decides he must let him know and hands him this note:
"Top of the Ninth, basses loaded."

A notoriously surly and boorish baseball umpire returns home after a long road trip. He settles into his easy chair and calls his little boy over to sit on his lap. "No," says the lad, "the son never sits on the brutish umpire."

A man comes home to find a notorious Czechoslovakian philanderer coming out of his wife's bedroom. He chases him down the hall, out the window, and down the fire escape.
On his way down, the philanderer jumps into another apartment and says to the surprised tenant, "Can you cache a small Czech?"

A Spanish mother and a Jewish father name their daughter Carmen Cohen. The mother only addresses her as Carmen and the father will only call her Cohen with the result that she never knew if she was Carmen or Cohen.

In order to forget his terrible hangover, a man goes hunting with his dog. Almost immediately, a large rabbit jumps out of the brush and grabs hold of the dog's leg with his teeth. The man shoots the rabbit and rushes home to stew it. The hangover disappears with the first bite, which was the piece of the hare that bit the dog.

All the top chess players arrive at a hotel for an international tournament. They spend the first hour or so standing around the lobby telling each other of recent victories. Without warning, the hotel manager throws them all out of the lobby and tells them to go to their rooms.

When asked why, he says, "If there's one thing I can't stand it's chess nuts boasting by an open foyer."

An Indian rajah becomes so selfish about hunting that he forbids all his subjects from the sport.

Angered, they rise up and overthrow him, making this the first time a reign was called because of game.

Scientists have found a tribe of half a thousand women in India who were born without nipples. Perhaps you've heard of them by their more common name: the India Nippleless 500.

A light-bulb manufacturer announces that he will give away free bulbs to any theater owner who uses them on his marquee.

"This is madness," says his accountant.

"I know, but I've always wanted to see my lights up in names."

Two servicemen in Africa are bragging about which is the better lion hunter. They bet a pint of beer on who will be the first to bag a lion. The first man sets off on foot while the second goes to a nearby air base, where he borrows a jet. The man in the jet sights a lion and shoots it.

As he claims his prize, he points out that a strafed lion is the shortest distance between two pints.

A hospital patient who had refused to have his temperature taken was finally asked by the head nurse why he would not cooperate. His answer: "On the springs, the young man's fanny politely spurns the shove."

Year in and year out, a doctor stops by a bar on the way home from work and orders a daiquiri with a walnut in it. One day the bartender sees the doctor approaching, reaches for a walnut, and finds that there are none. He rushes around the bar until he finds an old hickory nut, which he tosses in the glass.

The doctor takes one sip, grimaces, and bellows, "What the hell is this?"

The bartender meekly replies, "A hickory-daiquiri, Doc."

The Milwaukee Brewers cannot win against Milt Famey, a pitcher who is normally mediocre but a terror against them. It is late in the season, and the Brewers need a win badly, but they are facing Famey the next day. They hit on a plan. One of the team's front-office men will arrive at Famey's hotel, pose as a fan, and try to get Famey drunk on beer. The plan works to the extent that Famey drinks ten bottles of beer with the "fan."

The next day, however, Famey is perfect through eight innings, and the Brewers' only solace is that the other team is also scoreless. Then in the ninth, Famey walks four successive batters, which eventually gives the Brewers a 1-0 victory.

Later in the locker room there is a toast: "Here's to Schlitz, the beer that made Milt Famey walk us."

"I would like to reaffirm my belief in Buddha," said the Oriental gentleman, "but there is a great deal to be said for margarine."

"Why is a leaking parking lot like the Frankenstein monster?"
"It's a porous car loft."

A professor of Greek takes his torn suit to a Greek tailor. The tailor looks at the pants and says, "Euripides?"

"Yes," replies the professor, "Eumenides."

"Eureka," someone shouted within earshot of Marx Brother Chico.

Glaring, he shot back, "You doan smella so good yourself."

A noted dog trainer gives a party in honor of his most talented animal, a spaniel. As part of the festivities, the spaniel sits down at a baby grand and begins playing a Bach sonata. During the recital, one of the guests begins to talk loudly, and the dog growls and chases the noisy guest out of the room.

"Don't worry," the trainer shouts nervously, "his Bach is worse than his bite."

A woman opened her refrigerator and spied a rabbit there.
Woman: "What are you doing in my icebox?"
Rabbit: "This is a Westinghouse, isn't it?"
Woman: "Yes."
Rabbit: "I'm just Westing."

"Terrible day," said the Great Dane as he complained to his master. "Work was bad, but then I got on the bus and it was completely packed with small dogs."

"Well," replied the master, "that's what you get for riding during peke hours."

"Dad, what is that over there underneath the funny-looking beast?"

"There's nothing, son, under the gnu."

Two racehorses, meeting at Santa Anita, eye each other for a moment.

"Don't I know you?" asks one.

"I think so. I don't recall your name, but the pace is familiar."

Two goats are busy eating garbage. One finds a roll of old film and chews it up.

"Did you enjoy the film?"

"Actually, I preferred the book."

"If your father could see you now," said the mother turkey to her errant son, "he'd turn over in his gravy."

[handwritten annotation: what did ... say]

Two frogs were sitting on a lily pad. One leaned over to the other and said, "Time sure is fun when you're having flies."

Two snakes are talking about the social airs being put on by an old acquaintance.

"Just think," says one, "I knew her back when she didn't have a pit to hiss in."

Two microbes become bored with life in the lymph system of a horse and move into the animal's blood system, where they are immediately killed by a dose of penicillin.

Moral: Don't change streams in the middle of a horse.

A dentist becomes completely obsessed by floss. His compulsion becomes so great that he buys a roan horse to help him gather floss for his growing collection. Another dentist becomes even more compulsive and steals the first man's horse, but the horse refuses to help him.

Moral: A stolen roan gathers no floss.

Three American Indian women were all preparing to have babies. To make them comfortable, the chief asked each one what kind of animal skin she wanted to bear her baby on. The first chose a bearskin, the second requested an elk hide, and the third asked for the hide of a hippopotamus.

They all gave birth. The first had a five-pound son, the second a six-pound son, and the third had an eleven-pound baby boy.

All of this goes to prove that the son of the squaw on the hippopotamus is equal to the sons of the squaws on the other two hides.

There once was this little snail who loved fast sports cars. He bought himself a red Porsche and painted a big red S on each door. One day while going down the highway at a hundred miles per hour, he was spotted by a state trooper, who said to his partner, "Brother, look at that S-car go!"

A Datsun owner finds that he needs a special cog for his car's engine. It is a very early model car, and he is told that he must have a cog specially built at the Datsun factory and must buy a minimum of 100 of them. Since the car won't work without the part, he reasons that he has no choice but to buy all 100 of them. So eager is he to get the cogs that he flies to Japan and brings them back with him in his lap. As the plane is crossing the United States, the pilot announces engine trouble and orders the passengers to jettison all extra weight. The man slips one of the cogs into his pocket and throws the other 99 overboard.

On the ground a farm couple is just sitting down to dinner. The wife looks out the window and says to her husband, "Look, Fred, its raining Datsun cogs."

A man is stricken with the oddest affliction: Whenever he breaks wind, it makes the sound "honda." He finally asks his doctor about it. The doctor exhausts all the references in the literature and is just about to conclude that there is no answer when he is hit with a brainstorm. "I will call Honda in Japan and talk to the company doctor."

The Japanese doctor says, "Check to see if your patient has a dental infection—an abscess."

The patient is checked, and sure enough there is an infection. It is treated and the affliction ends.

But the American doctor is haunted by the ability of his Japanese counterpart to diagnose the problem from such a distance and finally calls him on the phone.

"Doc, how did you know?"

"Simple," replies the Japanese doctor. "Abscess makes the fart go 'honda.' "

In ancient Greece, Zeus visits a young man named Benny and tells him he can be immortal if he agrees to remain unshaven.

"If you shave," says the king of the gods, "you will burn and your ashes will remain forever in an urn."

All goes well for centuries, but one day in the twentieth century Benny falls in love with a woman who insists that he shave.

He figures that Zeus has forgotten by now and shaves. The ancient curse is immediately carried out.

Moral: A Benny shaved is a Benny urned.

Mercy Hospital in Chicago is run by a group of nuns, originally from Australia. Over the years, they have gone out of their way to maintain ties with their native land—for instance, there is a gigantic map of Australia in the main reception area, and they serve Australian tea from tins with koala bears on the outside.

One night a patient calls in the head nurse to let her know how much he loves the hospital.

"Sir, are you trying to tell me that there is nothing here that you don't like?" she says.

The man thinks for a moment and finally says, "Things are so good here that the only thing that I can complain about is the fact that I got some leaves in my tea the other night."

"Ah," she replies. "The koala tea of Mercy is not strained."

A gent named Tate invented a compass. It was a very sophisticated thing based on a new theory of magnetism. It went on sale at all the fancy sporting good stores and was in all the outdoor catalogs. Far and wide people were buying what had come to be called Tate's compass. Suddenly, it was discovered that the compass was notoriously unreliable. After that it became a maxim of outdoor life that he who has a Tate's is lost.

A man becomes totally fed up with his mean and vicious horse and shoots him. He sells the flesh, but finds nobody will buy the bones. He rows the bones out to the center of a lake. Just as he is about to dump them, a wind blows up, capsizes the boat, and the man drowns.

Moral: People who live with cross horses shouldn't row bones.

The monastery was having its annual smelt fry with beer, chips, and all the trimmings. A stranger stopped in the hopes of getting a bite to eat, and asked the first man he saw, "Are you the fish friar?"

"No," the brother answered, "I'm the chip monk."

A famous actor was attending the public cremation of a close friend when he was accosted by a fan who kept asking him annoying questions. To get away from the pest, he began to run; but he stumbled and fell into the fire. Recovering from his burns in the hospital, he remarked, "Just one more case of going from the prying fan into the pyre."

Julius Caesar is sitting in his tent, when Brutus bursts in and shouts: "Hail! Hail! Hail! Oh Mighty Caesar!"

Caesar rises with a start, and shouts back: "Brutus, how dare you hail while I'm reigning?"

Julius Caesar orders Brutus to get him a dozen apples. He soon returns and hands the apples to Caesar. On counting them,

Caesar finds only ten. Angrily he turns to Brutus and snarls, "ET TU, BRUTE?"

What is dracula's favorite dish?
The quiche of death.

After scientists perfected the cloning technique, they decided that each person should have a copy, which would be stored until the original person died, at which point the copy would carry on.

At first it was decided that the clones would be made in alphabetical order. However, many people without relatives argued that they should have priority so that they could carry on their names. The scientists decided this was fair and decreed, "Let him who is without kin stash the first clone."

An aging movie actor who has always done his own stunts decides it is time to get a stand-in and hits on the novel idea of getting a clone of himself.

Secretly, and at great cost, he has it done. The plan is a great success as the clone takes all the risks and bruises.

However, one day the actor is surprised when the clone bursts into his penthouse apartment swearing and yelling at him. The actor tries to calm the clone, but to no avail. Finally the clone becomes so agitated that he physically attacks the actor. The actor deftly stops the attack and manages to cause the other man to fall off the penthouse balcony to his death.

Ten minutes later a police officer arrives and tells the actor that he is under arrest.

"Arrest for what?" asks the actor. "That was not a real person, hence the charge of murder will not obtain. Try and charge me!"

The police officer thought for a moment, and then said, "I've got it: I'm charging you with making an obscene clone fall."

A man in a beret is sitting on a train, and a bear is sitting next to him. The bear is nodding off. A man across the aisle strikes up a conversation with the man in the beret and asks about the beast. It seems that the man in the beret is French and he is traveling across North America with his trained bear act. The two men get into an involved conversation when, suddenly, the bear starts to move around and growl. The Frenchman reaches into his bag and pulls out a large hypodermic needle with which he jabs the bear. The bear immediately nods off.

"Why did you do that?" asked the Frenchman's new friend.

"I have found, monsieur, zat zere is safety in numb bears."

· 6 ·

Too Much Saxon Violence

At the time this book was started, there were certain pun forms that were not immediately apparent to the author, but were suggested by others with a better ear for what was classic.

The missing/extra letter proverb. Jeffrey H. Goldstein, professor of psychology at Temple University and coeditor of *The Handbook of Humor Research* and *The Psychology of Humor*, finds it impossible to leave common phrases alone. Here are some that he has modified by a single letter:

> *Home is where you hang your cat.*
> *Home is where the heat is.*
> *Love is ever having to say you're sorry.*
> *A fool and his monkey are soon parted.*
> *You can't make a money out of me.*

Possibilities are endless, just as they are with *Little-known Towns.* The late Russell J. Dunn, Sr., of Lakewood, Ohio, played for many years with a number of formats including this one:

Shapeless, Mass.
Goodness, Me.
Deathly, Ill.
Praise, Ala.
Proan, Conn.
Inert, Mass.
Nohitznorunzno, Ariz.
Deeba, Cal.
Nevah, Mo.
Goinga, Ga.
Ether, Ore.
Sayno, Mo.
Hezmakinizatme, Pa.

Ooola, La.
Income, Tex.
Hittor, Miss.
Coco, Colo.
Farmerina, Del.
Noaz, Ark.
Lowe, Cal.
Acapel, La.
Sweetasapls, Ida.
Doremifaso, La.
Sheza, Tenn.
Carr, Wash.

Dunn also worked with a variation on that format: Troy a little tenderness, Helena hand basket, Billings and cooings, Topeka out of the torn sock, Spokane like a gentleman, Orlando the free, Fairbanks pay interest, Cheyenne never has a date, Utica like a watch, Boise stupid, and Juneau the way to San Jose?

There were other examples, but clearly the most habit forming was a new form from the fertile mind and files of an Illinois woman named N. Sally Hass. One would be hard pressed to find a better example of the "degenerative pun" than these that take their cue from this simple question and answer:

Why did they ban The Story of O?
  Too much sex and violence.

Degeneration then sets in.

Why did they ban *Ivanhoe?*
  Too much Saxon violence.

TOO MUCH SAXON VIOLENCE

Why did they ban the story of the compulsive eater who sold germ-contaminated secondhand microscopes to finance his addiction?

Too much snacks and vile lenses.

Why did they ban the story of the mother who worked her fingers to the bone knitting hosiery to pay for her son's music lessons?

Too much socks and violins.

Why did they ban the story of the 13 drunken interior decorators who managed to hang the wrong color drapery fabric over every single window frame of a 42-room mansion?

Too much soaks and valances.

Why did they ban the story of the doctor who cured the soprano's laryngitis by having her massage her throat with VapoRub and refrain from singing a note or speaking a word for an entire month?

Too much Vicks and silence.

Why did they ban the story of the spoiled-rotten princess who stood at her window for three days and pouted at the mobs of upper-grade serfs who were attacking the castle?

Too much sulks and villeins.

Why did they ban the story of the mental health facility where half the patients insisted that they were really Charlie (The Bird) Parker and the other half went around all day muttering, "Where are the snows of yesteryear?"

Too much sax and Villon.

Why did they ban the story of the mother fox who was so jealous and possessive of her cubs that every time one of them went out on a date, she would surreptitiously sabotage his appearance by sneakily sticking bits of dandelion and milkweed fluff to his coat?

Too much vixen's sly lints.

Given such a display, it is hard to resist adding one's own. Here's mine:

Why did the National Football League attempt to discourage overly macho razor-blade ads that featured professional football players?

Too much Schicks and virilence.

In 1987 a courageous man named Jeffrey S. Sawtelle of Burke, Virginia, came forth with no less than eight important variations; to wit and in his exact words:

Why did the TV network censor a scene in *Death of a Salesman* in which Willy Loman complains about the lower back trouble, aches and pains, and bedbug bites he has acquired in his long career on the road from sleeping in too many bad beds in crummy motels?

Too much sacks and vile inns.

Why did the health authorities raid a sleazy motel upon receiving a report that it was vastly overcrowded with recent immigrants from India?

Too much sikhs in vile inns.

Why did the night clerk in a cheap motel suspect that the couple who registered dressed in expensive clothing from an exclusive upscale New York department store was hiding out from the cops?

Too much Sachs in vile inns.

Why did the TV network pull the plug on a football game in which the quarterback on one team was continually being tackled before he could get the ball off because two of his teammates had taken bribes from gamblers to throw the game and were therefore letting opposing players through?

Too much sacks and vile ends.

Why did customs officials arrest a string quartet upon discovering small plastic bags full of suspicious-looking white powder stuffed into nooks and crannies of their instruments?

Too much sacks in viol ends.

Why wouldn't the TV network run a documentary on Jim Jones and Jonestown?

Too much sects and vile ends.

Why wouldn't they book a concert by the Mantovani orchestra made up of church custodians?

Too much sexton violins.

Why were authorities concerned about a report that a laboratory was experimenting with test tubes full of deadly and contagious viruses?

Too much sicks in vial ends.

All of this suggests many other possibilities for the dedicated, degenerative punster. "Nothing is certain but death and taxes," in the mouth of an owl becomes ". . . death and taxidermists" for openers. One can turn a line like "A sad but excusable slip of the tongue" into a major piece of foolishness. A friend suggests the song "*Guantanamera*" as a gold mine of sung punch lines ("One-ton tomato," "Wantin' to mate oh," "Wanton tomato," etc.). For the world-class punster, there is the challenge of the next chapter.

· 7 ·

The Chattanooga Challenge

J okes with kickers or punch lines that rely on punned titles and lines from well-known songs are hardly uncommon, as shown by these fine examples:

A witch doctor tells one of his patients that the only cure he can suggest for the man's stomachache is to take a leather thong, cut it into twelve equal pieces, and swallow one each day.

Twelve days later he returns. "It's no use, Doc. The thong is gone, but the malady lingers on."

Tina, the Hollywood agent, was so upset by her inability to find work for a singer that she began to sob for her in her presence.

Her client tried to console her. "Don't cry for me, Agent Tina."

As fine as these are, however, they pall in comparison to the jokes that rely on a line from the song one reporter once said "very nearly became America's second national anthem during World War II."

It all started in 1974, when Glenn Collins of the *New York Times* got wind of a new joke form. He valiantly tried to find its source. He recalls today, "Never could track it down. Went through three people and tracked it to someone's teen-age son, who couldn't remember where he heard it." Remarkably, nobody has yet stepped forward to take credit for this discovery.

With the help of the *Times* advertising columnist Philip H. Dougherty, who had tipped Collins to this important joke phenomenon, a major collection was assembled and published in the *New York Times Magazine* of January 19, 1975.

Collins thought that it would become an overnight sensation and today seems a bit disappointed that his craze "seems to have left no residue."

His disappointment may be ill founded, however. This joke collector keeps finding evidence that Collins's work had a profound influence on some dedicated punsters who still try to come up with stories that end with a play on the line "Pardon me, boy, is this the Chattanooga Choo-Choo?" One devotee, Dr. Howard F. Heller of Omak, Washington, points out that the challenge is not for everyone:

"With most formula jokes most people groan and try to top the last joke (as opposed to just groaning) but the Chattanooga Choo-Choo joke is rarely tackled by those who hear it. One in a hundred might try."

There is other evidence that the struggle continues. In May 1983, an appeal for these jokes was broadcast on radio station WIND in Chicago by Norman Mark. There were a number of duplicates and slight variations on known versions as well as several new ones.

Here are 8 from Collins's original collection, plus 15 later versions of which the last 12 emerged from the punning and fertile mind of Jeffrey S. Sawtelle of Burke, Virginia.

1. According to a wholly unsubstantiated rumor repeated in White House circles shortly after former President Nixon retired to his San Clemente estate, it seems that only hours after his arrival in California, Mr. Nixon telephoned Gerald Ford. When the new president got on the line, Mr. Nixon is unreliably reported to have said:

"Pardon me, boy, this is the chap who knew to choose you."

2. As he was leaving the zoo, a visitor walked by the gnu cage and noticed an unkempt gnu sitting morosely in a corner. Outside the cage was a large bamboo shoot with teeth marks on it. Thinking the gnu might have thrown it out of the cage, the visitor turned to an attendant and said:

"Pardon me, boy, is this the shoddy gnu's bamboo shoot?"

3. (This is unquestionably the most popular example.) Roy Rogers, cowboy star, finally took delivery of his long-awaited pair of custom boots—made with crocodile skin inlaid with silver and precious stones. Roy had never before had such a pair of boots, and he'd owned 1,276. Slipping them on, he decided to give them a trial ride on the range. As he rode, he kept looking from right to left, admiring the beauty of his footware.

Suddenly an angry cougar leaped from behind a huge boulder. With a single swipe of his claws, the cougar shredded Roy's left boot. Leaping out of the saddle, he killed the cougar with his bare hands, threw the dead animal over the saddle, and returned angrily to the ranch house.

His ever-faithful wife, Dale, standing on the porch, immediately sized up the situation and exclaimed:

"Pardon me, Roy, is that the cat that chewed your new shoe?"

4. A tourist from Tel Aviv walked into an ornate chapel maintained by Vishnu Maharishi, an up-and-coming young New Delhi faith healer famous for his talkativeness. The Israeli visitor pointed at a gilt-edged bench in front of the chapel, and asked a nearby attendant:

"Pardon me, gou, is this the chatty new guru's pew?"

5. On the set of a new *Thin Man* movie, a prop man noticed Myrna Loy carrying a swatch of material in her hand. Said he:

"Pardon me, Loy, is that the shantung that's the new clue?"

6. Lamont Cranston, renowned crime fighter, was actually a secret candy-bar freak. One Saturday he went into his dressing room to satisfy his sweet tooth, and made a beeline toward his hidden cache of candy bars. There he spied his usually faithful Chinese manservant munching happily on something, and said with annoyance:

"Pardon me, Toy, is that the Shadow's nougat you chew?"

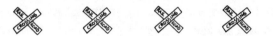

7. A new patient, one Mrs. L., was ushered into the office of Sigmund Freud in nineteenth-century Vienna. At first Mrs. L. was ill at ease in the presence of the great man, and extremely hesitant about explaining her troubles. Dr. Freud suggested that she lie down on the couch and say anything, whatever came into her head. Mrs. L., relaxing despite herself, started to talk, at first haltingly. Then, speaking compulsively, she found herself revealing her single greatest fear—that she was going crazy.

Suddenly, feeling terribly self-conscious, Mrs. L. stopped in midsentence, looked over at the great doctor, and said:

"Pardon me, Freud, but is my chatter really cuckoo?"

8. This one is so long it must be abbreviated: An unprecedented pan-Eastern dinner was held some years back, which was hosted by Premier Chou of China and included Nguyen Van Thieu of Vietnam. After watching the Chinese leader put away one nut-and-spice dish after another, one of the leaders turned to the Vietnamese leader and asked,

"Pardon me, Nguy, how many cashews did our Chou chew?"

9. A man had a favorite hat that he had worn for many years. Recently, however, the brim had been loosened in an accident,

and the man had been obliged to effect repairs with glue. The day after he had fixed the hat, he had a lunch date with a friend at a Chinese restaurant and, since it was a cold day, he wore a hat. As they were sitting at the table—the man with his hat in his lap—his friend accidentally spilled soy sauce across the table and onto his hat. The friend said,

"Pardon the soy, is that the hat you put the glue to?"

10. Not to be outdone by the "Snap, crackle, pop!" of the cereal industry, a confectionary chemist invented a candy that talks when you bite into it. So if you hear the words "Yummy, yummy, slurp, slurp, I'm so good" coming from the mouth of a chomping youngster, you can ask,

"Pardon me, boy, is that the chatty nougat you chew?"

11. Don Pardo, the famous announcer of "Saturday Night Live" fame, became incensed by the continued exploitation of the endangered naugha, which is brutally hunted for its hide. First he formed "Friends of the Naugha," and then to demonstrate his love of the little beast, he decided to raise a spirited naugha pup as a pet. After several years of care and feeding, he thought it might be a good idea to take it back to the vet who had originally examined it when it was a newborn. The vet took one look at the animal and exclaimed,

"Pardo, my boy, is this what the little naugha grew to?"

12. The maitre d' at a fancy restaurant gets one whiff of the fish of the day and puts out the word that he is banning it because it has gone bad.

Later, one of the busboys passes by with what appears to be a half-eaten portion of the fish. He stops him and asks:

"Pardon me, boy, but is this the shad I meant to taboo?"

13. Warren G. Harding, Jr., son of the president of the same name, bought a new Dusenberg automobile and was driving it down Constitution Avenue when it had a flat tire, pulled to the right and into a tree, and was demolished. The president, seeing what had happened, walked up, looked at the ruined tire, and said,

"Harding, my boy, is that the flat that slew your new Duse?"

14. An Irish policeman was sent to investigate a fire. He emerged from the burnt-out building with a fedora in one hand and a revolver in the other hand, and was heard to say to his young assistant:

"Arson, me boy. This hat and gat will do for new clues."

15. Yogi Bear decided to get his little bear buddy a car so that they could get around Jellystone Park more easily to steal picnic baskets. Ranger Smith, seeing it, queried:

"Pardon me, bear, is that the Datsun you got Boo-boo."

16. Walter Brennan, in his TV role as head of the Real McCoys, in one episode went into town to Louie's tattoo parlor to get himself tattooed. Little Luke, seeing it, said:

"Grandpa McCoy, is that the tattoo you had Lou do?"

17. A wine distributor, who had the exclusive franchise on an exclusive French vintage, was informed that an American counterfeit was on the market. So he set out to find out where it was being made. He looked long and hard and was getting discouraged, when, footsore and weary, he peeked into a warehouse and saw bottles of the fake stuff. Happy because his long search was over, he turned to the warehouseman and said:

"Pardon my joy: is that the *chateau neuf* you brew, too."

18. Myrna Loy, famous film actress of yore, once played a ballerina. She was shooting her big scene when her costume began to come apart. Time was crucial, so, rather than have it sewn up, she

improvised by using some gooey baby food to hold her costume together until the shooting could be completed. Later, she took the dress to be cleaned, and the clerk, seeing the gooey spot on the dancing dress, said:

"Pardon me, Loy, is that the pap that glued your tutu."

19. A landlord was put on trial for negligent homicide. It was charged that he failed to provide adequate heat for an apartment, causing the tenant to freeze to death. The landlord replied that the loss of heat was due to defects in the design of the apartment, which he could neither foresee nor control, and, in any case, the deceased brought it on himself by walking around naked in the middle of the winter. The landlord was convicted, but his mother appealed to the governor, saying:

"Pardon my boy. It was the flat that slew the nude dude."

20. Thomas Hardy, the novelist, got a shipment of new bottles of wine. He left one bottle out, only to find that a pack rat stole it and took it to his nest, which was reached by going down a stove pipe. A friend of Hardy's tracked the rat to its nest, recovered the bottle, and brought them to the writer, saying:

"Hardy, my boy, is that the rat who flued your new booze?"

21. The pastor of a small church was upset because a boys' Sunday school class meeting in the sanctuary was getting rowdy and out of hand, and the kids were tearing up the furniture. He planned a small party for them, with candy and other refreshments, at which time he intended to have an informal talk with them and—charitably, of course—bawl them out. Concerned about how to tactfully word this so the boys would take the hint but not be too offended, he worked long and hard on his remarks. His loving wife, seeing him emerge from his study, notes in hand, said:

"Parson, my joy, is that the chat 'n' nougat pew chew?"

22. Foy Willing and the Riders of the Purple Sage once battled a mob of outlaws who hid out in a local slough, riding out from there to steal and plunder. Since the boys were outnumbered, they had to use strategy. A fat cowboy who worked for the band worked out a trap. The outlaws were tricked into a hole where they were buried in a mountain of cow pies, buffalo chips, and similar material that demoralized and rendered them easy to catch. Willing was under the impression that another cowboy, a skinny one, had thought up the plan, and was giving him all the credit, when someone sidled up to him and said:

"Pardon me, Foy, the fatty's that who pooed the slough crew."

23. Hardin and Weaver, a locally famous and long-established team of Washington, D.C., radio disc jockeys, at one point in their career decided to form a fan club. They announced it over the air and invited people to join and pay dues. The initial response was not very good. Eventually, Hardin and Weaver decided to turn over their club and its treasury to a jazz musician of their acquaintance. He wasted all the money and left town. The incident was reported to the police, who arrested a suspect and invited the guys down to identify him. Weaver, on seeing the lineup, wasn't sure, so he turned to his partner and said:

"Hardin, my boy, is that the cat who blew our few dues?"

· 8 ·

Here Come the Elephants

They first lumbered onto the scene in early 1963, building on prototypes that had been kicking around for years. ("What did Tarzan say when he saw the elephants?" "I don't know, what did Tarzan say?" "Here come the elephants.")

Time magazine immediately termed them ". . . an escape from an overlogical and overmechanical world." Later, in an article in the *Journal of Popular Culture,* they were said to have arrived "just in time to save a country which was up to its neck in earnestness and involvement, on the one hand, and wretched political satire . . . on the other." Perhaps.

Then as now, their appeal lay in large, relentless doses; to tell just one or two is to miss the whole point. They also tend to work better if you are between the ages of 9 and 15. It was no fluke that the best of elephant-joke books—*101 Elephant Jokes*—was written by Robert Blake, 14, who ran the following warning at the beginning of his work: "Practically no parents will think elephant jokes are funny."

But all of this is quite irrelephant; bring on the jokes.

How much did the psychiatrist charge the elephant?
   Thirty-five dollars for the visit and $350 for the couch.

What is gray, has short antennae, large wings, a long nose, and gives money to elephants?
   The tusk fairy.

How do you get down from an elephant?
   You don't get down from an elephant, you get down from a goose.

Why do elephants live in the jungle?
   Because it is out of the high-rent district.

What's the similarity between an elephant and a grape?
   They're both purple, except for the elephant.

Why do elephants drink?
   They want to forget.

Why does an elephant have cracks between his toes?
   To carry his library card.

What did the elephant do when he broke his toe?
   He called a toe truck.

What did the grape say when the elephant stepped on it?
   Nothing, it just let out a little whine.

Why do elephants have wrinkled ankles?
   They lace their sneakers too tightly.

What did the banana say to the elephant?
   Nothing. Bananas can't talk.

Why don't elephants like martinis?
Have you ever tried to get an olive out of your trunk?

How do you get an elephant out of a tub of Jell-O?
Follow the directions on the back of the box.

How can you prevent an elephant from charging?
Take away his credit card.

How do you make an elephant float?
Take two scoops of ice cream, an elephant, and some root beer.

Why do elephants wear sneakers?
To creep up on mice.

How can you tell if an elephant has been in your refrigerator?
From the footprints in the butter.

What's the difference between an elephant and peanut butter?
The elephant doesn't stick to the roof of your mouth.

Why do elephants have trunks?
Because they don't have glove compartments.

What do you call it when an elephant sits on a fence?
Time to buy a new fence.

Why did the elephant paint his toenails different colors?
So he could hide in the M&M's.

What's gray on the inside and clear on the outside?
An elephant in a Baggie.

What does an elephant call a dinosaur?
Extinct.

What has two tails, six feet, and three trunks?
    An elephant with spare parts.

If there were three elephants in the kitchen, which one would
be the cowboy?
    The one on the range.

What weighs two thousand pounds and is covered with lettuce
and mayonnaise?
    A Big McElephant.

Why are there no elephants in Hawaii?
    Because they can't afford the air fare.

What do you do with an elephant with three balls?
    Walk him and pitch to the giraffe.

What do you get when you cross an elephant and a prostitute?
    A three-quarter-ton pickup.

Why did the elephant sit on the marshmallow?
    So he wouldn't fall into the hot chocolate.

What do you get when you cross an elephant and a mouse?
    Dunno, but it sure makes big holes in the walls.

How do you get an elephant out of your bathtub?
    Pull the plug.

What is gray and powdery?
    Instant elephant.

What do you find between elephant's toes?
    Slow-running pygmies.

What has twelve legs, is pink, and goes, "Bah, bah, bah?"
    Three pink elephants singing "The Whiffenpoof Song."

What is gray and stamps out jungle fires?
    Smokey the Elephant.

What is Smokey the Elephant's middle name?
    The.

What's convenient and weighs twelve thousand pounds?
    An elephant six-pack.

What did the drunk elephant say to the second drunk elephant?
    Don't look now, but is that a pink human?

How can you tell if there are elephants under your bed?
    You can touch the ceiling with your nose.

What's covered with fur, has a long trunk, and loves peanuts?
    An elephant in a mink coat.

What has big ears, weighs two thousand pounds, and has two trunks?
    An elephant going on vacation.

Why aren't elephants allowed on beaches?
    Because they can't keep their trunks up.

What weighs four thousand pounds and sings?
    Harry Elefonte.

What's black, covered with feathers, and weighs two thousand pounds?
    An elephant that's been tarred and feathered.

Why don't many elephants go to college?
    Few finish high school.

What's red on the outside and gray on the inside?
    Campbell's cream of elephant soup!

How do you get an elephant out of the theater?
    You can't; it's in his blood.

What did the elephant say to the naked man?
    How the heck do you drink with a thing like that?

What happens to old elephant jokes?
    They fall flat.

Elephant jokes begat a string of like absurdities:

Banana Jokes

What do you call a banana in prison?
    A convict.

What do cannibals eat for dessert?
    Bawana splits.

Grape Jokes ⭐ ⭐

What do you call great bodies of water filled with grape juice?
    The Grape Lakes.

What's purple and goes buzz, buzz, buzz?
    An electric grape.

What's the largest thing ever made of grapes?
    The Grape Wall of China.

What's small, purple, and dangerous?
    A grape with a submachine gun.

What's large, purple, and lies across the ocean?
    Grape Britain.

Tomato Jokes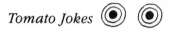

What's red and goes up and down, up and down?
A tomato in an elevator.

Why didn't the tomato go to the dentist?
Tomatoes don't have teeth.

How do you fix a broken tomato?
With tomato paste.

What's red, runs on batteries, and costs six million dollars?
The Bionic Tomato.

Plum Jokes ✪ ✪

What noted plum wrote under an assumed name?
Nom de Plum.

How do you tell a plum from an elephant?
A plum always forgets.

What do you call an eight-hundred-pound plum with a nasty temper?
Sir.

Gorilla Jokes ◉ ◉

Why did the ape wear blue suspenders?
His red ones broke.

What's the best way to call a mean gorilla?
Long distance.

Monster Jokes ★ ★

How does a monster count to 14?
On his fingers.

What do sea monsters eat?
Fish and ships.

How do you train King Kong?
Hit him with a rolled-up newspaper building.

There is no end to all of this, and anyone who thinks this absurdist fad is over hasn't been within earshot of a schoolyard in recent years.

· 9 ·

Said Swiftly

They are, for lack of a better term, high-speed puns. Some of us love them for just that reason—no story, no buildup, just quick formulaic hits best delivered in relentless salvos. From a larger field here are five twentieth-century examples starting with a form, admittedly sexist by today's standards, which became popular in the 1920s and continued strong until the end of World War II.*

She Was Only a . . .

. . . artist's daughter, but what a crowd she could draw (or,
. . . but she knew where to draw the line).

* These were still popular in my neighborhood in the late 1940s and fully half of those listed here were dredged from the crevices of my brain, where they had been stored for all that time. When they started pouring forth, I finally figured I may have failed geometry in the seventh grade because my brain was too cluttered with such things to make room for theorems.

. . . attorney's daughter, but what a will to break.

. . . blacksmith's daughter, but she knew how to forge ahead.

. . . bottlemaker's daughter, but nothing could stop her.

. . . boxer's daughter, but she knew when to faint.

. . . carnival queen, but she made a lot of concessions.

. . . censor's daughter, but she knew when to cut it out.

. . . chauffeur's daughter, but she could shift for herself.

. . . chimney sweep's daughter, but she soots me fine.

. . . coal dealer's daughter, but, oh, where she had bin.

. . . conductor's daughter, but she told you where to get off.

. . . convict's daughter, but she certainly knew all the bars.

. . . doctor's daughter, but she knew how to operate.

. . . electrician's daughter, but she went haywire.

. . . fruit-store owner's daughter, but, oh, what a peach.

. . . golfer's daughter, but her form was perfect.

. . . governor's daughter, but what a state she was in.

. . . graph maker's daughter, but she knew where to draw the line.

. . . hash slinger's daughter, but how she could dish it out.

. . . horseman's daughter, but she didn't know how to say nay.

. . . jockey's daughter, but all the horsemen knew her.

. . . judge's daughter, but she could dispose of any case.

. . . milkman's daughter, but she was the cream of the crop.

. . . minister's daughter, but you couldn't put anything past her.

. . . moonshiner's daughter, but I love her still.

. . . parson's daughter, but she had her following.

. . . poet's daughter, but I've seen verse.

. . . plumber's daughter, but, oh, those fixtures.

. . . prizefighter's daughter, but she certainly knew all the ropes.

. . . quarryman's daughter, but she took everything for granite.

. . . railroader's daughter, but her caboose was the talk of the town.

... realtor's daughter, but, oh, what development.

... sergeant's daughter, but she knew when to call a halt.

... shoemaker's daughter, but she gave the boys her awl and stuck to the last.

... surgeon's daughter, but, oh, what a cutup.

... taxi driver's daughter, but you auto meter.

... telephone operator's daughter, but she had good connections.

... waitress's daughter, but she sure could dish it out.

... window dresser's daughter, but she was no dummy.

Daughters were finally eclipsed by:

Oldies

On April 19, 1951, General MacArthur delivered his farewell address to a joint session of Congress. As part of his farewell, he quoted a line from an old song—"Old soldiers never die, they just fade away"—and a new formula was born.

First came the puns:

General Dye retired and moved to a small seaside town called Faye, where he spent many hours wading in the surf. An old comrade visited him, and came back to report to his friends, "Old Dye never soldiers, he just wades at Faye."

And then came these:

Old bathing beauties never die, they just wade away.

Old crapshooters never die, they just fade away.

Old gardeners never die, they just spade away.

Old hairdressers never die, they just braid away.

Old teachers never die, they just grade away.

Which, in turn, were followed by these:

Old accountants never die, they're just disfigured.

Old auctioneers never die, they just look forbidding.

Old ballplayers never die, they're just debased.

Old botanists never die, they're just deflowered.

Old brick layers never die, they just throw in the trowel.

Old cardiologists never die, they just lose heart.

Old committee members never die, they are just disappointed.

Old fishermen never die, they just smell that way.

Old generals never die, they are just debased.

Old glaziers never die, they just have a lot of panes.

Old grammarians never die, they only parse away.

Old helicopter pilots never die, they just lose their choppers.

Old housewives never die, they just wash away.

Old janitors never die, they just kick the bucket.

Old lawyers never die, they just lose their appeal.

Old mathematicians never die, they are just nonplussed.

Old orchestra leaders never die, they are just disbanded.

Old pickpockets never die, they just steal away.

Old poker players never die, they are just discarded.

Old postal workers never die, they just become unzipped.

Old railroad workers never die, they just get derailed.

Old sign painters never die, they just let go.

Old skiers never die, they just go downhill.

Old songwriters never die, they just decompose.

Old tree surgeons never die, they are just uprooted.

Old washing machine operators never die, they just keep agitating.

This type of pun enjoys periodic, limited revival, although the exact format changes. A more recent incarnation came in one of Elaine Viets's 1981 columns in the *St. Louis Post-Dispatch*. A reader sent her a quote by Virginia Ostman, which appears in the book *Peter's Quotations* and asks,

If lawyers are disbarred and clergymen defrocked, doesn't it follow that electricians can be delighted; musicians denoted; cowboys deranged; models deposed; tree surgeons debarked and dry cleaners depressed?

Viets and her readers rose to the occasion and supplied a number of *de-* and *dis-*words for various professions. Here are some of those findings augmented by contributions from the fertile mind of Russell Dunn, Sr.

Bankers	discredited	Packers	desecrated
Butchers	delivered	Photographers	developed
Caped crusaders	dismantled	Pig farmers	disgruntled
Celebrities	defamed	Poker players	deduced
Citizens	devoted	Preachers	decreed
Curtain makers	depleted	Reporters	depressed
Dentists	decayed	Sightseers	detoured
Detectives	dissolved	Sleepers	debunked
Fishermen	debated	Songwriters	decomposed
Grammarians	denounced	Students	detested
Hair stylists	distressed	Teachers	degraded
Magicians	disillusioned	Telephone	
Married women	dismissed	operators	disconnected
Mathematicians	deciphered	Vegetarians	decelerated
Moonshiners	disconcerted	Weavers	defrayed

Adverbial Abuse

The premise was based on a quaint and obvious mannerism used in the original Edward L. Stratemeyer Tom Swift books: to have an adverb match what Tom was saying. Although others had played with adverbial puns before, it was not until the early 1960s that it became a fad with a name. They were called Tom Swifties by three San Franciscans—Paul Pease, Bill McDonough, and John

Larrecq—who hit on the idea of a series of books immortalizing such lines as "What our ball club needs is a man who can hit 60 homers per season," said Tom ruthlessly, and "My commute ticket expired," said Tom extraneously.

Like all fads, the Tom Swiftie fad had its time, but there still are those who continue to collect and concoct adverbial puns. The collection assembled here (which also includes several *verbal* puns) contains, among others, more than a hundred from Mike Weber and Caroline Bryan of Milwaukee. (I'd mention the company they work for, except that it looks as though they used the company's computer for this important work, and it's possible the company's other work would look trivial by comparison). Additionally, dozens more were provided by the late Russ Dunn.

Not only is this one of the longest lists of adverbial puns ever assembled, but because of the work of Weber, Bryan, and Dunn it is compiled alphabetically by adverb from "abashedly" through "wryly"—a major breakthrough for those who need a quick match for "high-handedly" or "vibrantly."

"I smashed up both my front fenders," she said abashedly.

"Nobody showed up," he replied absently.

"Okay, wise guy, I'll splash some on your clothes" was his acid reply.

"You will pay for eating that apple," God said adamantly.

"And 15 more baseball gloves," he admitted.

"I will let you in without a ticket," he admitted.

"I can't think of any more poetry," she said adversely.

"Uh-oh, I'm out of fuel," said he aghast.

"But who is flying this airplane?" he asked airily.

"They're bringing me back to life!" said Tom animatedly. (This line was used as a lead to an April 16, 1991 *Wall Street Journal* article on the revival of Swift in a new series of books.)

"Let's buy some of that fresh fruit," she said with aplomb.

"No, I don't know the name of the Roman god of the sun," he apologized.

"Is that a Picasso?" he asked artfully.

"They just stole all my paintings," she said artlessly.

"Yes, I'll buy that perfume," he assented.

"I'm trying to do something about my bad breath," he asserted.

"No, officer, I was sitting here on my backside," he asserted.

"I must judge how well he cut the donkey loose," he asseverated.

"I am Lord High Executioner of the guillotine," he asseverated.

"This exam is the toughest of the year," he attested.

"Yes, you may copy from the book I wrote," he authorized.

"This is power steering," he said automatically.

"You, my friend, are losing your hair," he stated baldly.

"Yes, I'm starring in a French movie," she barely blurted out.

"Feed your dog," his father barked.

"Ulp, I just swallowed a fish lure," said he with bated breath.

"I'm glad you got your headlight fixed," she beamed.

"Blow on the fire and it will burn better," he bellowed.

"Fan that fire faster!" the blacksmith bellowed.

"My bed isn't made," he complained in a blanket statement.

"I love reading," she said bookishly.

"I am awfully sunburned" was her blistering remark.

"Don't be an ass," Tom brayed.

"What? Fly into this hurricane?" he cried breezily.

"Where is the lamp?" she asked brightly.

"See my new camera?" he asked candidly.

"Let's send these packages to the poor overseas," she said carefully.

"This acid will *really* clean your silverware," she replied caustically.

"Household tasks can be fun," he chortled.

SAID SWIFTLY

"Right this way, Charles," she chuckled.

"Let's get our whole family together at a secret place," he said clandestinely.

"I have just washed all your windows," she spoke out clearly.

"Which of these @#%&* classes should I take?" he asked coarsely.

"C'mon, have another soda," he coaxed.

"I haven't started painting yet," he remarked colorlessly.

"She flew with us," she complained.

"Take the prisoner below," said the captain condescendingly.

"I did it with the actor Mr. Parker," she confessed.

"Our sockets are overloaded," she declared confusedly.

"I am going to join the Trappists," he said contemplatively.

"We've reached the South Pole," he remarked coolly.

"But I do not know Mr. Geiger," he countered.

"Do you play golf?" he would ask as a matter of course.

"Will you marry me?" he asked with courtly gestures.

"I'm going to stay away from the Brahma bull," the rider said, cowed.

"This Model T Ford never starts," the mechanic said crankily.

"I've dropped my toothpaste," he stated crestfallen.

"I became rich through oil," he boasted crudely.

"Can you crack this code?" she asked cryptically.

"Let's begin the operation," the doctor said cuttingly.

"I can't see in this closet," he hinted darkly.

"That will be $400," the mortician said with deadly precision.

"I had a flat tire," he said somewhat deflatedly.

"The fog is too thick to drive in," she said densely.

"The horse just shrugged, and he fell right off," she derided.

"This is the Venus de Milo," the guide said disarmingly.

"I can speak for myself," said the Queen of Denmark, disdainfully.

"I am one hip guy," he said disjointedly.

"I did my best to take the puzzle apart," she dissembled.

"Delilah has cut my hair!" said Samson, somewhat distressed.

"Well, I'll be an SOB," he said doggedly.

"I think your canines need training," she said dogmatically.

"Not another pineapple diet," she said dolefully.

"This is the last money I'll shell out for this wedding," the bride's father said dourly.

"Watch out for that hive in the tree," she droned.

"There's too much vermouth in my martini" she said dryly.

"I have no thoughts on the new waterfowl legislation," he said ducking the issue.

"Piece o' cake," she replied effortlessly.

"Do you think I needed all those vitamins?" he asked energetically.

"I accept your proposal," she replied engagingly.

"Stay away from that precious ancient urn," she pleaded evasively.

"Yes, father, we lost our mine to that prospector," she exclaimed.

"That dessert will destroy my diet," she expanded richly.

"I just flew in from the Coast," he explained.

"There's 16 ounces in that bag," she expounded.

"Hey, watch where you're going on the turnpike!" he shouted expressly.

"I feel dizzy," she whispered faintly.

"I feel so good after going to church," he said faithfully.

"I just love baby animals," she said fawningly.

"Take this mink coat, my love," the lover said fervidly.

"Take my temperature," he said feverishly.

"I always salute the Stars and Stripes," he bragged flagrantly.

"Columbus will fall off the edge of the earth," he said flatly.

"Uh-oh, a blowout," he said flatly.

"It's the Navy," he said fleetingly.

"Is the tumbling act still in town?" he asked flippantly.

"Let's play tiddledywinks," she said flippantly.

"What good is French money?" she asked frankly.

"My wallet fell out during the dance," he said frugally.

"We are going to have a record harvest this year," he said fruitfully.

"I smell gas," he fumed.

"Do you play tennis?" he asked gamely.

"I hope we bag a rhino," he said gamely.

"This large piano costs $5,000," proclaimed the musician grandly.

"I'll see if I can dig it up," he said gravely.

"I find fairy tales depressing," she said grimly.

"Look out for the bear," he yelled in a grisly voice.

"No one gets past this gate," the officer said guardedly.

"They have stabbed me through," she said halfheartedly.

"I have clubs, diamonds, and spades," she said heartlessly.

"Well, I'm not exactly finished trimming the bushes," she hedged.

"Please, teacher, may I leave the room?" she asked high-handedly.

"I've won the daily double," he cried hoarsely.

"We will burn your embassy," they cried hotly.

"Faith and charity are my only good qualities," he said hopelessly.

"Mush!" the Eskimo shouted huskily.

"And tear down the Stars and Stripes," they said unflaggingly.

"Alter your course: glacier up ahead!" he responded icily.

"Nobody wants my services anymore," the doctor said impatiently.

"This is the chicken-pox ward," the nurse said infectiously.

"I just adore this new mink coat," she inferred.

"I don't have a penny to my name," he said innocently.

"She's my parents' daughter," he insisted.

"You know, this magnet really works!" he said ironically.

"Oh, that crummy poison ivy," she said irritably.

"I've lost my rare Chinese brooch," she said jadedly.

"Who cares that the bouquet is missing a flower," said the bridesmaid lacadaisically.

"When can I take this cast off?" he asked lamely.

"The plumbing in the White House needs repair," the reporters leaded.

"No, sir, there are no hills on this road," said the gas station attendant on the level.

"There's a bathroom on every floor," said the real estate agent levelheadedly.

"Let us all raise our champagne in a toast," she said with lifted spirits.

"Then you suck this hose from the helium tank," he said lightheadedly.

"They ain't gonna take me alive," said Long John Silver limply.

"Uh-oh, I forgot what to get at the store," he said listlessly.

"I wish I were taller," she said longingly.

"This coat is at least two sizes too large," she said loosely.

"What's wrong with orange plaid?" he asked loudly.

"I'm the janitor around here," he maintained.

"Put prices on all merchandise," he said markedly.

"So many aggies and cat's-eyes in the deluxe set!" he marveled.

"I must get back to the store," she said, minding her own business.

"I can't milk this cow," he said moodily.

"Very talkative cats you have there, ma'am," he mused.

"Where will I get inspiration for my ode?" she mused.

"I'll get even with that lousy hound," he muttered.

"We hung out our flag on the Fourth of July," he observed.

"Hey, watch where you're cutting," he said off-handedly.

"I'd say your pants are too short," the tailor said off the cuff.

"It's a nice Christmas tree," she opined.

"I've born 11 children," she boasted overbearingly.

"What a rotten hand you've dealt me," said the bridge player in passing.

"Are you a doctor?" she asked patiently.

"What vegetable goes with carrots?" she asked peacefully.

"I get *Time, Newsweek,* and *U.S. News,*" he would say periodically.

"Better brush your shoes clean," he persuaded.

"Darling daughter, you've been on the phone for an hour," he said phonetically.

"I don't like the mountains," she said plaintively.

"I'm taking harp lessons," the student said pluckily.

"Get that pin off my chair," she demanded pointedly.

"This will break our budget," he explained poorly.

"All our rooms are filled, sir," said the clerk with a preoccupied air.

"Hello, class, I am your teacher," she professed.

"Psst! Your next line is on the cue card," he said promptly.

"Isn't that a peculiar reaction?" the scientist queried.

"Stop! I'm alive," she yelled quickly.

"Take any seat you like," he said randomly.

"Get out of these headwaters," she cried rapidly.

"It's the measles," the doctor diagnosed rashly.

"That mirror was a real good investment," he said upon reflection.

"Sorry, we can't pick up your garbage," he refused.

"Oh, no, my mother-in-law is coming," he said, relatively annoyed.

"I had to regrade those essays," she remarked.

"I didn't really send that telegram twice, did I?" she cried remorsefully.

"I have to glue these sheets of wood back together," he replied.

"The chorus must sing again," she required.

"The only other lodge is a hundred miles from here," said he as a last resort.

"Fishing and swimming in the summer, skating in the winter," he responded.

"We're going to have leftover cutlets tonight," she revealed.

"Stop the music!" he rhapsodized.

"I'll hit you with my best punch," he said righteously.

"Hey, I'm weightless," said the astronaut, rising to the occasion.

"My ball landed somewhere on the fairway," the golfer said roughly.

"Our carpet has really taken a lot of wear," she said ruggedly.

"There are 12 inches in a foot," the judge ruled.

"This tractor is quite weather beaten," he said rustically.

"My dear wife has left me," he cried ruthlessly. (Or, "I don't believe in sex therapists on television," she said ruthlessly.")

"There's a lot of cactus on this prairie," she observed sagely.

"Yes, dear, I always have hollandaise on potatoes," she said saucily.

"Get your hands off the oven," she screamed scorchingly.

"I'll have to look for it," he replied searchingly.

"We've just survived another earthquake," she said, visibly shaken.

"I broke your glasses" was her shattering statement.

"This wool *is* pretty low quality," she said sheepishly.

"How do you like my petticoat?" she asked shiftlessly.

"I can't find my glasses," he said shortsightedly.

"Honey, will you *please* stop nagging me?" he asked shrewdly.

"Do you want laughing gas while I drill?" the dentist asked smilingly.

"Hurry up and take my picture," he snapped.

"You've mussed my hair!" she snarled.

"This is pretty bad candy," she snickered.

"You've got a pretty big nose," he said snootily.

"I like this new toilet tissue," she said softly.

"He stabbed me through," he said sordidly.

"Aha, but you have signed your afterlife away," the devil said soulfully.

"The price for these lemons is ridiculous," she said sourly.

"You'll need this for your bike wheel," he spoke.

"We try to keep our Christmas trees fresh," he said sprucing up.

"We're about to run out of gas," he sputtered.

"Ug. You-um be Thunder Cloud's wife," he squawked.

"Alabama, Alaska, Arizona, Arkansas . . ." she stated.

"Pipe down," the steamfitter shouted.

"Let's stay ahead of the other boat," the captain said sternly.

"I can't help laughing over my operation," said he in stitches.

"There is too much starch in this shirt," he said stiffly.

"What's that bird with the long beak?" the little girl asked stoically.

"Rats, it's going to rain again today," he stormed.

"The house is right up ahead," he said straightforwardly.

"That tree trunk wasn't there last night," she said, stumped.

"So for homework, learn these arithmetic tables," the teacher summed up.

"I am going to keep all my money," he surmised.

"I have just sat on some upholstery nails," he said tactfully.

"I don't *have* to do this for a living," she said tartly.

"Call me a cab!" he bellowed taxingly.

"The revenue people are after me again," he replied taxingly.

"My dentures nearly fell off the cliff," she said with teeth on edge.

"You gave me two less than a dozen," he said tensely.

"Keep your eyes on your own exam," the teacher said testily.

"I've got a lot of things on my mind," she asserted thoughtfully.

"Yes, we're going to have an earthquake," he averred with a tremor.

"See my new sports car?" he asked triumphantly.

"We can form a monopoly with this merger," they declared trustingly.

"But I *do* work in a pretzel factory," he thought in his twisted mind.

"Don't tell me I'm out of hash," he growled uncannily.

"This plane is about to crash!" he sobbed uncontrollably.

"I got all D's on my exams," she would cry unfailingly.

"My hand is numb," she said unfeelingly.

"Sorry, there is no guarantee with this one," was the unwarranted reply.

"I am insane," he said unwittingly.

"You must be Kareem Abdul-Jabbar," he spoke up.

"Aw, go milk a cow," she uttered.

"I see Dudley cut classes again," she commented vacantly.

"Quit feeling my pulse!" he shouted in vain.

"I have just learned to play the xylophone," he said vibrantly.

"I love to see happy dogs," she said waggishly.

"I told you that you'd get stung," he said waspishly.

"How do you like the hair piece," he inquired wigishly.

"But I've always lived just west of England," he wailed.

"Chinese food excites me," she said wantonly.

"Here is the fourth Timex I have found this week," she said watchfully.

"Oh, how I hate long good-byes," she wavered.

"Our paper comes out four times a month," he said weakly.

"Aren't five cups from one tea bag too much?" she asked weakly.

"I'm glad I did well on my EKG," he said wholeheartedly.

"You won't get a penny from me when I die," he said willfully.

"My horse won't stop," he shouted woefully.

"I can't imagine what happened to those loaves of bread," he wondered.

"What kind of bread should I bake?" the baker asked wryly.

Do Its 👉

The most recent outbreak of the disease caused by the same virus that brought on the Tom Swiftie epidemic has come in the "do it" form. It all started with a few T-shirts and bumper stickers proclaiming such truths as: "Nurses do it with patience" and "Teachers do it with class." They proliferated, and the highways were soon turned into a forum for professional/sexual puns. No matter that some were forced—"Dancers do it with their feet" and "Potters do it with clay" don't exactly cater to mainstream fantasies—the fad has created some great bumper-to-bumper reading.

The nation's leading collector/creator of "do its" is Dr. Reinhold Aman, editor of *Maledicta: The International Journal of Verbal Aggression.* Aman has collected enough to have published a book of them (available from Maledicta Press, 331 South Greenfield Avenue, Waukesha, Wisconsin 53186). Here is a small selection from his much larger recollection:

Admirals do it fleetingly.
Anesthesiologists do it unconsciously.
Artisans do it craftily.

Bankers do it interestingly.
Beginners do it startlingly.
Belgians do it bilingually.
Ben does it gaily.
Bigots do it intolerably.

Californians do it sharingly.
Camels do it humpingly.
Cannoneers do it ballistically.
Canoeists do it with their paddles.
Cardiologists do it heartily.

Catholics do it rhythmically.
Chicagoans do it breezily.
Chinese do it inscrutably.
City slickers do it urbanely.
Clockmakers do it watchfully.
Columnists do it regularly.
Compulsives do it neatly.
Computer operators do it bit by bit.

Defense attorneys do it objectively.
Dentists do it inextricably.
Dermatologists do it flakily.
Dogs do it cynically.
Dolphins do it flippantly.
Donkeys do it asininely.
Drill operators do it boringly.
Drinkers do it spiritually.
Drummers do it differently.

Editors do it with consistency.
Einstein did it relatively.
Electronics engineers do it unbiasedly.
Elephants do it with their trunks.
Emperors do it majestically.
Engineers do it mechanically.
Eunuchs do it uniquely.
Exhibitionists do it flashily.
Experts do it authoritatively.

Felines do it cattily.
Field marshals do it strategically.
Frankenstein did it monstrously.
Frenchmen do it frankly.

Germans do it markedly.
Gibbons do it swingingly.

SAID SWIFTLY

Gillespie does it dizzily.
Grammarians do it punctually.
Gregory did it enchantingly.

Hairdressers do it permanently.
Helen does it readily.
Henry did it thoroughly.
Hotheads do it quickly.

Illiterates do it indescribably.
Indian guides do it unerringly.
Ivan did it terribly.

Jacob and Wilhelm did it grimly.
Johnny Carson does it four times a week.
Journalists do it reportedly.

King Arthur did it nightly.
Knights do it boldly.

Lawbreakers do it offensively.
Lensmakers do it objectively.
Libertines do it freely.
Louisianans do it bayoutifully.

Magicians do it inexplicably.
Mailmen do it zippingly.
Masturbators do it singlehandedly.
Mathematicians do it figuratively.
Michelangelo did it on his back.
Miners do it with their shaft.
Monoglots do it unilingually.
Motorists do it exhaustingly.
Mountaineers do it condescendingly.
Musicians do it harmonically.
Myopics do it shortsightedly.

Nouveaux riches do it upwardly.
Nudists do it barely.

Oil refinery workers do it crudely.
Omahans do it mutually.

Paranoids do it suspiciously.
Painters do it with even strokes.
Philosophers do it questionably.
Pigs do it sloppily.
Poles do it with polish.
Printers do it without wrinkling the sheets.
Procrastinators do it later.
Professors do it testily.
Prostitutes do it tartly.

Rabbits do it hairily.
Railroad engineers do it tenderly.
Reporters do it sensationally.
Roosters do it cockily.
Rulers do it measuredly.

San Franciscans do it shakily.
Schizophrenics do it twice.
Semioticians do it symbolically.
Septuagenarians do it weakly weekly.
Shriners do it conventionally.
Skeptics do it incredibly.
Spies do it under cover.
Statisticians do it averagely.
Studs do it polysemously.
Sycophants do it praisingly.

Tautologists do it repeatedly.
Thespians do it playfully.
Thieves do it stealthily.
Tom does it swiftly.
Triplets do it thrice.

SAID SWIFTLY

Truckers do it wrecklessly.
Trumpeters do it hornily.
Twins do it doubly.

Undertakers do it gravely.

Venus de Milo did it unarmedly.
Violinists do it unstrungly.

Wagnalls does it funkily.
Washingtonians do it diplomatically.
Whores do it trickily.
Widows do it lamentably.
Witch doctors do it charmingly.
Writers do it literally.

· 10 ·

Operknockety Tunes

In the early days, the vast majority of knock-knocks were lines from songs, which meant you got to sing the fifth line. To some purists, these are a separate art form and should never be mixed with the other types. Here they are, then, in a separate hoard. Many date back to the Big Band Era.

Knock, Knock.
    Who's there?
    Aardvark.
    Aardvark who?
    Aardvark a million miles for one of your smiles.

OPERKNOCKETY TUNES

Knock, Knock.
    Who's there?
    Agatha.
    Agatha who?
    Agatha world on a string.

Knock, Knock.
    Who's there?
    Akron.
    Akron who?
    Akron give you anything but love, baby.

Knock, Knock.
    Who's there?
    Amahl.
    Amahl who?
    Amahl shook up.

Knock, Knock.
    Who's there?
    Ammonia.
    Ammonia who?
    Ammonia bird in a gilded cage.

Knock, Knock.
    Who's there?
    Annie.
    Annie who?
    Annie thing you can do, I can do better.

Knock, Knock.
    Who's there?
    Apocryphal.
    Apocryphal who?
    I've got Apocryphal of dreams.

Knock, Knock.
Who's there?
Barrymore.
Barrymore who?
Barrymore not on the lone prairie.

Knock, Knock.
Who's there?
Barton.
Barton who?
Barton up your overcoat.

Knock, Knock.
Who's there?
Bay.
Bay who?
Bay be face, you've got the cutest little baby face.

Knock, Knock.
Who's there?
Barry.
Barry who?
Barry me not on the lone prairie.

Knock, Knock.
Who's there?
Big Horse.
Big Horse who?
Big Horse of you.

Knock, Knock.
Who's there?
Caesar.
Caesar who?
Caesar jolly good fellow, Caesar jolly good fellow.

OPERKNOCKETY TUNES

Knock, Knock.
    Who's there?
    Crimea.
    Crimea who?
    Crimea river. I cried a river over you.

Knock, Knock.
    Who's there?
    Darrell.
    Darrell who?
    Darrell never be another you.

Knock, Knock.
    Who's there?
    Deirdre.
    Deirdre who?
    Deirdre mother come from Ireland?

Knock, Knock.
    Who's there?
    Dexter.
    Dexter who?
    Dexter halls with boughs of holly.

Knock, Knock.
    Who's there?
    Domino.
    Domino who?
    Domino thing if you ain't got that swing.

Knock, Knock.
    Who's there?
    Domino.
    Domino who?
    Domino cowhand.

Knock, Knock.
>Who's there?
>Don Ameche.
>Don Ameche who?
>I'll be Don Ameche in a taxi, honey.

Knock, Knock.
>Who's there?
>Don Juan.
>Don Juan who?
>I Don Juan to set the world on fire.

Knock, Knock.
>Who's there?
>Donna.
>Donna who?
>Donna sit under the apple tree.

Knock, Knock.
>Who's there?
>Ferry.
>Ferry who?
>Ferry tales can come true.

Knock, Knock.
>Who's there?
>Frankfurter.
>Frankfurter who?
>Frankfurter memories.

Knock, Knock.
>Who's there?
>Freeze.
>Freeze who?
>Freeze a jolly good fellow.

Knock, Knock.
  Who's there?
  Gnome.
  Gnome who?
  Gnomebody knows the trouble I've seen.

Knock, Knock.
  Who's there?
  Greta.
  Greta who?
  Greta long, little dogie, greta long.

Knock, Knock.
  Who's there?
  Hal.
  Hal who?
  Hallelujah! I'm a bum.

Knock, Knock.
  Who's there?
  Heifer.
  Heifer who?
  If Heifer I should lose you.

Knock, Knock.
  Who's there?
  Humus.
  Humus who?
  Humus remember this, a kiss is just a kiss.

Knock, Knock.
  Who's there?
  Hyman.
  Hyman who?
  Hyman the mood for love.

Knock, Knock.
　Who's there?
　Igloo.
　Igloo who?
　Igloo Susie like I knew Susie.

Knock, Knock.
　Who's there?
　Ivy League.
　Ivy League who?
　Ivy League for every drop of rain that falls, a flower grows.

Knock, Knock.
　Who's there?
　Jimmy.
　Jimmy who?
　Jimmy that old time religion.

Knock, Knock.
　Who's there?
　Jose.
　Jose who?
　Jose can you see by the dawn's early light?
　(This can also be accomplished with O'Shea.)

Knock, Knock.
　Who's there?
　Karloff.
　Karloff who?
　Karloff my dreams, I love you.

Knock, Knock.
　Who's there?
　Keir Dullea.
　Keir Dullea who?
　On a Keir Dullea you can see forever.
　(Ina Claire was used in earlier versions.)

Knock, Knock.
  Who's there?
  Kelly.
  Kelly who?
  Kellyfornia, here I come!

Knock, Knock.
  Who's there?
  King Kong.
  King Kong who?
  King Kong the witch is dead.

Knock, Knock.
  Who's there?
  Lima Bean.
  Lima Bean who?
  Lima Bean working on the railroad.

Knock, Knock.
  Who's there?
  Llama.
  Llama who?
  Llama Yankee doodle dandy.

Knock, Knock.
  Who's there?
  Marcus Welby.
  Marcus Welby who?
  It Marcus Welby spring.

Knock, Knock.
  Who's there?
  Mary Lee.
  Mary Lee who?
  Mary Lee we roll along.

Knock, Knock.
Who's there?
Navajo.
Navajo who?
You'll Navajo just how much I love you.
(See also, Yule.)

Knock, Knock.
Who's there?
Mean Tummy.
Mean Tummy who?
Why must you be Mean Tummy?

Knock, Knock.
Who's there?
Offenbach.
Offenbach who?
I have Offenbach on this street before.

Knock, Knock.
Who's there?
Oil Can.
Oil Can who?
My Oil Can Tuckey home.

Knock, Knock.
Who's there?
Olaf.
Olaf who?
Olaf my heart in San Francisco.

Knock, Knock.
Who's there?
Pettygil.
Pettygil who?
A Pettygil is like a melody.

Knock, Knock.
  Who's there?
  Picasso.
  Picasso who?
  Picasso you there's a song in my heart.

Knock, Knock.
  Who's there?
  Piranha.
  Piranha who?
  Piranha old gray bonnet . . .

Knock, Knock.
  Who's there?
  Sam and Janet.
  Sam and Janet who?
  Sam and Janet evening.

Knock, Knock.
  Who's there?
  Rapunzel.
  Rapunzel who?
  Rapunzel your troubles in your old kit bag.

Knock, Knock.
  Who's there?
  Shelby.
  Shelby who?
  Shelby coming around the mountain when she comes.

Knock, Knock.
  Who's there?
  Somber.
  Somber who?
  Somber over the rainbow.

Knock, Knock.
    Who's there?
    Sonia.
    Sonia who?
    Sonia shanty in ol' shanty town.

Knock, Knock.
    Who's there?
    Sony.
    Sony who?
    Sony a paper moon.

Knock, Knock.
    Who's there?
    Swedish.
    Swedish who?
    Ida, Swedish apple cider.

Knock, Knock.
    Who's there?
    Tarzan.
    Tarzan who?
    Tarzan Stripes forever.

Knock, Knock.
    Who's there?
    Theresa.
    Theresa who?
    Theresa nothing like a dame.

Knock, Knock.
    Who's there?
    Underwear.
    Underwear who?
    Underwear my baby is tonight?

Knock, Knock.
    Who's there?
    Venue.
    Venue who?
    Venue vish upon a star.

Knock, Knock.
    Who's there?
    Wendy.
    Wendy who?
    Wendy moon comes over the mountain.

Knock, Knock.
    Who's there?
    Yule.
    Yule who?
    Yule never know just how much I love you.

· 11 ·

Shaggy Dog Show

These jokes are very hard to categorize. In his important *Esquire* essay on the subject, J. C. Furnas concluded that "shaggy dog" is the only label that fits—*goofy,* for instance, is too broad, while *pointless* is too derogatory. Although he had no label for them, Furnas was able to describe the best of them as ". . . classics which, once heard, stick in the mind like taffy in a dog's jaw and are beautifully calculated to outrage people who can see nothing funny in them at all." Bennett Cerf, another shaggy dog expert, was content to define them by example: ". . . tales in which animals talk, humans do inexplicable things, and the punch line makes no sense at all."

But if they are hard to label, they are a delight to tell. Eric Partridge, the great expert on the English language, actually wrote a book entitled *The Shaggy Dog Story,* in which this point is made as well as it will ever be.

The "shaggy dog" story does indeed represent the acme of the storyteller's art, for it demands a wittily unexpected and sudden ending, all the more unexpected in that the "lead-in" and the "lead-up" have had to be deceptively leisurely and almost diffuse; it demands also a considerable skill in narrative. . . . However absurd it may be, a "shaggy dog" must never be silly.

Although they have been divided in other ways, I am convinced that they fall into three natural categories: (1) stories about animals, (2) stories not about animals, and (3) stories about animals in bars.

In order to get as many of these as possible into the pages ahead, I have tightened them some. So when they are retold, you may want to embellish them a little to give them that "deceptively leisurely" quality Partridge mentioned.

Also, two rules should be observed when telling them: (1) Never say in advance that you are going to tell a shaggy dog story, as this will detract from the absurdity of it all, and (2) animals at bars almost always order martinis—the only other acceptable animal drink is a Manhattan. No other form of life, not even a parrot, would ever order a strawberry daiquiri.

🐾　　🐾　　🐾　　🐾

Stories About Animals

This, according to Bennett Cerf and a number of others, was the prototypical tale first told in the early 1940s.

During the Great Depression, a recently unemployed man in New York sat on a park bench, idly scanning a copy of the *London Times*. His eye fell upon an elegantly set advertisement for a lost shaggy dog, promising a "substantial reward." Shortly afterward he saw just such a dog, an Old English sheepdog, and collared it. Despite his dwindling resources, he bought a steamship ticket for himself and a space for the dog on a fast ocean liner, sailed for Southampton with anticipation, put dog and himself into a London train, and finally took a taxi to the Belgravia address shown in the ad. With the dog sitting beside him on the front steps, he rang the doorbell. After an appropriate pause the door opened, disclosing a butler in full regalia. Our hero said, "You advertised, I believe, for a lost shaggy dog." The butler looked down at the dog disdainfully, and remarked, "But not so shaggy as that, sir." He then closed the door.

(The following, on the other hand, is a recent example of the art.)

A traveler was driving through Arkansas when he lost his way and got off the main highway. In a short time, he found himself driving along a narrow, bumpy, back-country road.

Just as he began to wonder whether he should turn back or drive on until he could find a place to ask directions, he crested a hill, and in the valley beyond was the biggest pig farm he had ever seen.

As he drove by, he saw rows and rows of pigsties and pigpens, and pigs running in fields and pigs wallowing in mud. Suddenly, his eye caught something really strange. He did a double take, muttered to himself, and then looked a third time. He wondered if he had seen correctly—it looked like a pig with a wooden leg!

He found the lane to the farmyard and drove up into the farmyard, where he was met by the farmer. "Excuse me," the traveler said. "I was just driving by and looking at all your pigs, and I noticed something that I just had to stop and ask about. Tell me, did I see right? Is there really a pig out there with a wooden leg?"

The farmer smiled. "Oh, that would be old Caesar you were seeing. He's the finest pig a man could ever hope to have—and smart! Well, let me tell you a little about that pig.

"You see that barge down there on the river? That's a mining dredge, taking out platinum ore. Old Caesar sniffed out the vein and showed us how to set it up. Now that dredge brings me in about $120,000 every year.

"Over there in the meadow, you see those oil derricks? It was Caesar who showed them where to drill. Of course, it is just a small operation, but I got a quarter of a million on the mineral lease, and each year the wells bring me in about $80,000 in royalties. See, I had Caesar negotiate the contract.

"Now, I can tell you are a city fellow, and you probably never thought of pigs as being particularly smart, much less intellectual, but old Caesar there, well, he has an honorary degree from the Sorbonne in Paris. Four or five times each year, Caesar travels off to various universities both here and abroad to give guest lectures on theoretical physics. The honoraria from those lectures bring me $20,000 or $25,000 every year, plus it is good advertising for the farm.

"There's another thing, a little more personal. One night a couple of years ago I got to drinking, and I guess I had more than I should have. I passed out drunk, fell down, and knocked over a lamp. That started a fire in the house, and old Caesar smelled the smoke. He came in the back door, got the wife and kid out, roused me up, and got me out. There is no question about it—that night old Caesar saved all our lives, and you know, that is not the sort of thing a man is going to forget too easily."

"Why," the traveler said, "this is all amazing! I have never heard of a pig like this before! This is fantastic! But tell me, how did he get that wooden leg? Was he in a wreck or something?"

The farmer laughed. "Well, naturally," he said, "when you have a pig that smart, you don't want to eat him all at one time."

A violinist believes that his music has become so captivating that he can now march into the deepest jungle and tame savage beasts by playing for them. He heads into the jungle, and the first thing that happens is that two lions are entranced by his playing of Mozart. A panther and a leopard draw close and join the audience. Suddenly, a hyena comes crashing through the underbrush, pounces on the violinist, and devours him, to the annoyance of the other animals.

"Why did you do a thing like that?" one of the lions says. "This man's music was magnificent, and just as we were really beginning to enjoy ourselves more than we have ever enjoyed ourselves before, you crash in here and destroy everything."

The hyena cups his paw to his ear, leans over closely to the lion, and shouts, "What say?"

One goldfish to his tankmate: "If there's no God, who changes the water?"

An ad appears in the paper asking for an individual who can type, take dictation, program a computer, and speak more than one language.

The first applicant for the job is a dog. The dog is able to type 145 words per minute, takes perfect dictation, and not only can program a computer but has written several programming manuals.

The prospective employer has the dog demonstrate all of these skills, and then turns to him and says, "I'm dazzled by your qualifications, so I only have one final question: What about the language requirement?"

The dog looks at him and says, "Meow!"

All but one of a prized flock of homing pigeons return to their coop, and the owner becomes very worried.

At three in the morning, the pigeon's owner is pacing the floor when he hears a tapping at the door. He opens it to find his lost bird, wet and bedraggled.

"What happened to you?" says the man.

"Well," replies the pigeon, "it was such a nice day I decided to walk."

"I have the greatest dog act," says the agent to the manager of a famous symphony hall.

"This isn't a circus," replies the manager.

"No, no, you don't understand. Bring the full orchestra into the hall and have the grand piano at center stage."

Reluctantly, it is done, and the agent then walks onto the stage with a small dog, who sits down and starts to play Grieg's Piano Concerto, flawlessly.

"This is the greatest thing I've ever seen," whispers the manager to the agent.

At that very moment, a larger dog strides onto the stage.

"Is that dog also in the act?"

"No," replies the agent. "It's the dog's mother. She wanted him to be a doctor."

Years ago, when the Dodgers were still in Brooklyn and Leo Durocher was the team's manager, a horse wandered up to the great manager and said, "Why don't you use me on your team, Leo? I can hit and field as well as anyone on your team."

"Get lost! I've got enough troubles."

"Come on, Leo, give me a chance—try me in the field."

"Okay, just for laughs."

The horse went into the field and made one spectacular catch after another.

"Amazing," said Durocher. "Come on in and bat."

The horse hit one ball after another over the fence, and Durocher signed the horse on the spot.

The next day, the Dodgers were playing the Giants. The first three Giants were put out by the dazzling fielding of the horse. The Dodgers came to bat and the first three men reached base. With the bases loaded the horse came to bat, and he blasted the first ball over the Ebbets Field wall.

"Run, run!" Durocher yelled, but the horse just stood there.

"Are you kidding?" said the horse. "If I could run, I'd be racing at Jamaica!"

"Carry your bag?" asked the redcap to the alligator about to board the plane for London.

"Sure, but be careful, that's my wife."

Two trained seals meet in their agent's outer office.

"It's terrible," said one. "Did you hear what happened to our old friend Fred?"

"What could it be? I heard that he finally got a job."

"That was the problem. He went to his first rehearsal, jumped in the tank, sank to bottom, and drowned. He'd been out of work so long he forgot how to swim."

A man is offered a magnificent horse at a very cheap price.

"What's wrong with him?" says the prospective buyer.

"Well, he has a strange habit. He sits down on grapefruit."

"I can live with that," says the buyer. "I'll take him."

A few hours later the buyer returns on foot. "I can't figure it out. I was riding across a stream and the horse sat down and still refuses to get up. I went into the water and felt around and couldn't find any grapefruit."

"Oh," says the seller, "I forgot to tell you he also sits down on fish."

"Somebody ate my porridge," bellowed Papa Bear.

"Somebody ate my porridge," cried Baby Bear.

"Oh, shut up," snapped Mama Bear. "I haven't even served it yet."

The electric eel in the aquarium became depressed, and his keeper asked if there was anything that could be done.

"I'm unhappy because I have no wife," said the eel.

The next day the keeper dropped a female eel into the tank, returned an hour later, and was shocked to find the male eel just as depressed as he had been before.

"What's the matter now?" he asked.

"Damn it," he said turning toward the intended mate, "DC."

Smith and Jones are on safari, and one night after dinner Smith bets Jones a dollar that he will be the first to shoot a lion.

"In fact," says Smith. "I'll do it right now." Smith heads off into the jungle.

An hour later a lion pokes his head inside the tent and says, "You know a guy named Smith?"

Trembling, Jones says, "Well, yes."

"He owes you a dollar."

A young American doctor saved a baby elephant's life while traveling through the African jungle. Many years later, the doctor finds himself in the most unenviable position: penniless, lost, and without a practice. One day he drifts into a small town, works for a few hours, and makes enough money to buy a drink and a cheap ticket to the circus, which is in town.

At the beginning of the circus, the elephants come out. The lead elephant recognizes the old doctor and trumpets his joy at seeing him. Without hesitation he wraps his trunk around the doctor, lifts him out of his two-dollar seat and plunks him down on one of the five-dollar seats.

A female zebra working as a reporter is traveling around the United States for a report she is doing on the status of American animals.

She runs into a stallion on a country road, pulls out her notebook, and asks, "And what is it that you do, sir?"

The stallion says, "Lady, take off those silly pajamas and I'll show you."

Two dachshunds were chatting.

"I can't figure it out," said the first dog. "I'm in perfect physical shape but I'm constantly anxious."

"Why don't you go to a psychiatrist?" said the second. "How can I? I'm not allowed on the couch."

A man buys a talking bird for his wife's birthday. It speaks seven languages and costs him a thousand dollars.

"Well, did you get the bird I sent you?" he asks that evening.

"Yes," says his wife. "I already have it in the oven."

"What! That bird could speak seven languages!"

"Then why didn't it say something?"

A missionary is chased through the jungle by a ferocious lion, who corners him. With no other option left, the missionary falls to his knees in prayer. To his great surprise, the lion also begins to pray.

"This is miraculous," says the missionary, "joining me in prayer when I had given myself up for lost."

"Don't interrupt," says the lion, "I'm saying grace."

Two horses, followed by the stable dog, are on their way to the starting gate.

Says one, "Pal, we've been stablemates for the last five years. Today is my last race, as I will retire tomorrow and become a stud. I know you're the favorite, but maybe you could let me win this one, as it will improve my possibilities as a stud."

Just then the little dog blurts out, "Aha, I've heard every word of this shameful proposition, and I'm going to report both of you to the trainer."

The second horse looks at the first horse and says, "Look, a talking dog!"

A traveling salesman arrives in a country store where he finds four men playing poker with a fox terrier. He becomes more amazed when he watches the dog call for two cards, raise his bet, and rake in the pot.

Finally he says, "That's amazing. I've never seen such a smart dog."

"He ain't smart," says one of the men at the table. "Whenever he gets a real good hand he wags his tail."

A man with a dog act went into a booking office. He had a Spitz and a fox terrier. The terrier would announce the act and tell jokes for a few minutes. The booking agent jumped up and said, "Wow, that terrier is terrific."

"No," said the owner, "the fox terrier is nothing. The Spitz is a ventriloquist."

A man with an interest in show business is walking down a country road and walks by a horse, which says, "Hello, sir, remember me? I won the Kentucky Derby five years back."

A bona fide talking horse, the man thinks as he runs to find its owner.

"That horse is no damn good," says the owner, "but if you really want him, you can have him for twenty dollars."

"Twenty?" the man retorts. "I'll give you two thousand." "Fine with me, but has that old haybag been giving you that malarkey about winning the Derby? I happen to know it was the Preakness, and he didn't even win."

Two sardines are discussing tennis, and one says, "I've got a great idea, let's go to Forest Hills this year."

"How would we get there?" says the second.

"On the Long Island Rail Road," says the first.

"What, and get packed in like commuters?"

"Won't you let me lead one of my own lives?" said the put-upon young cat to its parents.

A worm coming out of the warm spring earth looked around and saw another worm looking at him.

"I love you," he said.

"Don't be silly, I'm your other end."

A man goes to the zoo and carefully positions himself close enough to one of the camels so he can drop a straw squarely on its back.

The camel turns his head. "Wrong straw."

A man in a movie theater notices what looks like a bear sitting next to him.

"Are you a bear?"

"Yes."

"What are you doing at the movies?"

"Well, I liked the book."

"It's cruel," said the papa bear to his family on seeing a carload of humans, "to keep them caged up like that."

"I've finally got him trained," said the first laboratory rat to the second. "Every time I go through the maze and press the bar he gives me a piece of cheese."

"Doc," says the leopard to his neurologist, "every time I look at my wife I see spots."

"That's quite normal."

"But you don't understand. My wife's a tiger."

A dog walks into a telegraph office, takes out a blank form, and writes, "Woof, woof, woof, woof, woof, woof, woof, woof, woof."

The clerk looks at it and says, "There are only nine words here; you could send another woof for the same price."

"But," the dog replies, "that would be silly."

A group of ostriches held regular meetings and were quite annoyed by Ostrich Bill, who was always late. Once they decided to play a trick on him and hide before he arrived. As they saw Bill approach, they all buried their heads in the sand.

Bill arrived, looked around, and said, "Well, well—I finally got here ahead of all of them."

Stories Not About Animals

A man staggers off the train obviously suffering from the worst sort of motion sickness.

"What happened?" his wife asks.

"Backwards . . . riding backwards . . . sick . . . makes me sick."

"My poor dear," she says, "but why didn't you ask the party sitting opposite you to change seats?"

"Couldn't," says the sick man. "There wasn't anyone there."

Aereo the Magnificent finally convinces a hard-bitten Hollywood agent to have a look at his act. He drags the agent to Madison Square Garden, which is set up for the circus that is just coming to town.

The performer takes off his robe, begins flapping his arms, and within moments is airborne. As he gains speed and altitude, he starts a dazzling show of trick aircraft maneuvers, including one in which he starts with a barrel roll, goes into a falling leaf, and regains power after dropping to within a foot of the floor. After 20 minutes of this, he lands in front of the agent.

The agent takes a puff on his cigar and says, "So what else do you do besides bird impressions?"

A company found that it could make a new and remarkable line of cosmetics from the skins of bullfrogs. Immediately it began advertising for frog skins, and one of the first replies was a telegram from a farmer in Texas who stated:

CAN SEND ANY QUANTITY UP TO 100,000. ADVISE.

A telegram was sent back asking for the full hundred thousand.

A week later a small box arrived from the farmer with one dried bullfrog skin and a note: "This is all there was. The noise sure had me fooled."

The man was bleeding profusely from the ear when he came into the emergency room screaming, "I bit myself, I bit myself."

"That's impossible," said the intern on duty. "How can a man bit himself on the ear?"

The man replied, "I was standing on a chair."

A magician shows his agent his new act in which he makes 200 cigars appear out of thin air, takes a puff on each, and then swallows them one at a time until they're all gone.

"That's amazing," says the agent. "How do you manage to do it?"

"Very simple," says the magician. "I get the cigars wholesale from a cousin in Tampa.

A man visits his elderly father, who lives alone in a small apartment above his store.

"Dad, I really worry about you. You work alone all day in the store and then come up here where you're alone. You really should develop some outside interests."

"Son," he replies, "it's not as bad as it looks. You see, I've got a hobby. I keep bees."

"You keep bees in this tiny apartment? Where could you possibly house them?" asks the son.

"There, over there on the table in a glass jar."

"But those bees will suffocate; that jar has a lid on it."

"What do I care?" says the father. "It's only a hobby."

"Number twenty-three," yelled the man from the bar at a nightclub. It was followed by a roar of laughter from around the room.

A newcomer asked one of the old-timers what was going on.

"Well it's like this, we've all been together for years, and we know each other's jokes. A while back we decided to compile a numbered list of our favorites, so that all you have to do is mention the number and everyone can recall the story."

"That's great," said the newcomer. "Let me see the list and try one out."

He looked at the list, spotted the funniest joke, and shouted out, "Number eleven!"

There was a deathly silence, yet he tried again. "Number eleven." The silence continued.

"Why did they laugh at twenty-three and not at eleven?" he asked the old-timer.

"Well, you see, " said the older man, "it isn't the joke so much as the way you tell it."

Each day at the end of office hours, a veterinarian stops at a bar for a drink. One day he notices that the owner's cat is getting fat. He examines the cat and tells him, "Pat, this cat is pregnant."

"Impossible," says the owner. "That cat has never been out of my sight."

Each time the vet comes in he repeats the diagnosis and each time the owner insists that the cat never had the opportunity.

One day the vet comes in and a huge tomcat walks out from under the bar.

"There, there," says the vet, "there's the father."

"Don't be silly," says the owner. "That's her cousin."

A traveling salesman knocked on the farmer's door late one night requesting a place to bed down.

"We're a mite tight on space," said the farmer, "so I'm going to have to put you in with my three sons."

"Pardon me," said the salesman, "I must be in the wrong joke."

A man who had gambled away every last cent in Las Vegas was forced to borrow a dime to use the rest-room pay toilet. When he got to the men's room, he found an unlocked stall and knew he had one last dime to use in a slot machine. He used the dime, hit the jackpot, and parlayed that jackpot into millions of dollars.

Now rich and famous, he went on a lecture tour telling his story and then declaring that if he ever found his benefactor he would split his fortune with him.

After he'd given his lecture a few thousand times, a man finally jumped up and declared, "I'm him. I'm the man who gave you the dime for the toilet."

"You're not the one," the lucky man shot back. "I'm looking for a guy who left the door open."

The old veteran had been given the job by the city of polishing the cannon in the civic center each day. When it came time for him to retire, they asked him what he was going to do with his leisure time, and he announced that he was going to buy a cannon and go into business for himself.

A newspaper reporter convinces the new circus midget to grant him a Sunday interview. The reporter arrives and a man close to six feet tall answers the door.

"I'm looking for Mr. Tiny."

"That's me."

"What?"

"I told you that this was my day off."

Animals at Bars

A man walks into a bar and orders two martinis: one for himself and one for his poodle. This goes on for a number of nights until one night the poodle comes in alone and says, "I'm sorry, my master isn't feeling well tonight, so perhaps you could give me my martini and he will pay for it tomorrow."

The bartender says fine and serves the dog his drink.

The next night the man and the poodle come in and the man says, "Thank you so much for being so kind to my poodle. In fact I've brought you a gift."

The bartender opens the gift box and finds a large, live lobster.

"Thank you, sir," says the bartender. "I'll take it home to dinner."

"Oh, she's already had her dinner," says the man. "Take her to a movie."

A grasshopper hops onto a bar, and the bartender turns to him and says, "Hi, little fellow, did you know that we serve a drink here that's named after you?"

The grasshopper looks at him with surprise and says, "You mean to say you have a drink named Irving?"

The bartender is startled as a great white shark slides through the door of his bar.

Sensing the bartender's consternation, the shark says, "It's okay Mac, I'm over twenty-one."

A man walks into a bar with a frog growing out of his ear.

"When did you first notice it?" the bartender asks.

"It started as a wart," replies the frog.

A rabbit and a lion come into a bar together and order martinis. The bartender puts out a bowl of peanuts, a bowl of popcorn, and a bowl of pretzels, which the rabbit begins eating. The lion just sips his martini.

"What's the matter?" asks the bartender of the lion. "Aren't you hungry?"

"Don't be silly," the rabbit answers. "If he were hungry, do you think I'd be sitting here?"

A man walks into a Third Avenue bar with his dog and orders two Manhattans: one for himself and one for the dog. Both knock back their drinks, eat the peels and cherries, chew up the glasses, and then spit the stems over their shoulders.

The process is repeated three times. Finally the man takes a look at the bartender, puts his arm around the dog, and says, "I bet you think we're crazy, don't you?"

"I sure do, the stem's the best part."

A gorilla walks into a bar with a banana tucked behind his ear. The bartender, a man of great restraint, decides he will not ask the gorilla about the banana because he figures it was placed there to get a rise out of him. Each day for 42 days the gorilla comes in with the banana and the bartender never mentions it.

Finally on the 43rd day the gorilla arrives with a carrot behind his ear. The bartender can't stand it any longer.

"Okay, what's the story with the carrot?"

"Couldn't find a banana today," the gorilla explains.

A man comes into a bar with a small white mouse in his pocket. He puts the mouse on the bar and orders a martini for himself and a thimbleful for the mouse.

After downing the drink, the mouse stands on its hind legs and sings a medley of songs from *My Fair Lady.*

The bartender is amazed.

"Listen," says the man, "buy us a round and you can keep the mouse."

The bartender serves the drinks and then says, "I can't believe that you're giving away a gold mine like that for a few drinks."

"Hell," says the mouse's former owner, "all he knows is *My Fair Lady.*"

A horse walks into a bar and orders a vodka martini, medium dry, shaken, not stirred.

A customer sits with his mouth open and his eyes agog while the horse sips the martini and chats with the bartender. After about 15 minutes the horse gets up and walks out.

"Did you see that?" says the customer.

"See what?" the bartender says.

"That horse," the guys says, "the one that came in here, ordered a vodka martini, and sat around chatting with you for 15 minutes. Don't you think that is a little unusual?"

"Yeah, now that you mention it," the bartender says, "he used to order gin martinis."

A well-known actor comes into a bar with a gorilla and two martinis are ordered.

The bartender then says to the actor, "Okay, what can he do—sing? tell jokes? dance? act? what?"

"Nothing," replies the actor.

"Then why did you bring him into this joke?" the bartender asks.

"He's my agent," says the actor.

An actor who had a trained dog act and was something of a ventriloquist found himself broke and far from home. Entering

a bar, he placed his dog on the stool next to him and ordered
a drink. As the bartender made the drink, the dog asked for a
martini.

"Who said that?" said the bartender.

"My dog," said the actor. "He can talk."

The bartender was fascinated, and while the man and dog had
their drinks, he chatted with them. Finally he said to the man,
"Your dog fascinates me. I'd like to buy him and I'll offer you
$100."

"Out of the question," said the man. "I'd want a lot more
than that."

The two dickered for a while and the bartender finally agreed
to pay the actor $350 in cash.

Just as the actor was getting up to leave, the dog turned his
head and said, "Wait a second, do I understand that you are going
to sell me to this man for a mere $350?"

"Yes," said the actor, heading for the door.

"Well," said the dog, "just for that, I'll never say another word
as long as I live."

Two ropes walk into a bar to get some drinks. The bartender
leans over to address the first rope, and asks, "Are you one of
them ropes?"

"Why yes," quavers the rope.

"We don't serve ropes here," says the bartender grabbing the
rope, twirling him around his head and throwing him out the
door.

The second rope decides that he had best disguise himself,
so he ruffles his threads and twists his two ends together.

Glaring, the bartender looks at the second rope and asks, "You
one of them ropes?"

"No," was the reply, "I'm a frayed knot."

A man trained his dog to carry an empty bucket to the corner
saloon and bring it back filled with beer. He paid for the beer

by tucking a dollar into the dog's collar. Not having a dollar one day, he tucked a five into the dog's collar.

When the dog did not return, he walked to the saloon and found the dog seated at the bar drinking a double martini.

"You never did anything like this before," said the dog's master.

"I never had the money before," replied the dog.

A lion walks into a bar and orders a dry martini. "What does a lion know?" thinks the bartender, and charges the lion ten dollars. After a while, the bartender's curiosity gets the best of him: He walks over to him, starts wiping the bar, casual-like, looks up, and says, "Say, you know, we don't get too many lions in here."

Says the lion, "I'm not surprised, at these prices."

A man enters a bar intent on a martini, when he notices that the bar is being tended by a horse in an apron.

" 'S'matter," says the horse as he drops an olive in the martini, "ain't ya ever seen a horse before?"

"No! No! It's not what you think," he says. "I'm just shocked that the cow that used to own this gold mine sold it."

· 12 ·

The Willies

Before there were sick jokes, there were Little Willies: compact, paired couplets filled with deep meanness. In his *Humor of Humor,* Evan Esar traced them back to 1899 and a sadistic little volume, *Ruthless Rhymes for Heartless Homes,* by an English poet named Harry Graham.

Graham's most famous rhyme:

> Billy, in one of his nice new sashes,
> Fell in the fire and was burned to ashes;
> Now, although the room grows chilly
> I haven't the heart to poke poor Billy.

Billy gave way to Willie, and hundreds of Little Willie quatrains began appearing and continued to show up in joke magazines through the 1950s. It is a shame that they have gone out of vogue. It is hard to find one that isn't a gem:

THE WILLIES

Willie saw some dynamite,
Couldn't understand it quite.
Curiosity never pays;
It rained Willie several days.

Willie, in his roguish way,
Pushed Grandpa into the fire one day.
Mother said, "My dear, that's cruel!
But of course it *does* save fuel."

Willie, with an awful curse,
Threw a saucepan at his nurse.
When he hit her on the nose,
Mother cried, "How straight he throws."

Willie split the baby's head,
To see if brains were gray or red.
Mother, troubled, said to Father,
"Children are an awful bother!"

Willie's cute as cute can be!
Beneath his brother, only three,
He lit a stick of dynamite.
Now Bubby's simply out of sight!

Into the cistern little Willie
Pushed his little sister Lily.
Mother couldn't find her daughter:
Now we sterilize our water.

Willie, hitting at a ball,
Lined one down the schoolhouse hall.
Through his door came Dr. Hill.
Several teeth are missing still.

Willie poisoned his father's tea;
Father died in agony.
Mother came, and looked quite vexed:
"Really, Will," she said, "what next?"

Little Willie hung his sister;
She was dead before we missed her.
"Willie's always up to tricks.
Ain't he cute? He's only six!"

Little Will, with Father's gun,
Punctured Grandma, just for fun.
Mother frowned at the merry lad:
It was the last shell Father had.

Willie took a pair of shears,
Cut off both the baby's ears.
At the baby, so unsightly,
Mama raised her eyebrows slightly.

Willie, looking down the gun,
Pulls the trigger "just for fun."
Mother says in accents pained:
"Willie is so scatterbrained."

Baby's in the ice-cream freezer.
Willie turns the crank to squeeze her.
Ma says: "Dear, the way that's fixed
You'll have that child completely mixed."

Willie, while the ice was thin,
Tried to skate and he fell in.
Willie tasted rather nice,
When they cut the pond for ice.

THE WILLIES

Willie stopped a cable car
While standing on the track.
It gave his system quite a jar—
His sisters now wear black.

Willie pushed his Aunt Elizer
Off a rock into a geyser.
Now he's feeling quite dejected—
Didn't get the rise expected.

Little Willie wrote a book;
Woman was the theme he took.
Woman was the only text.
Ain't he cute? He's oversexed.

Little Willie killed his sister,
A thing a brother should not do.
Cried his mother: "Now you'll catch it,
You've spoiled your father's brand-new hatchet!"

Little Willie, with a rock,
Beaned the cuckoo in the clock.
Father said: "Why don't it tick?"
Willie said: "The bird is sick."

He shot at Lee Wing,
But he winged Willie Wong;
A slight but regrettable
Slip of the tong.

Our Willie studied chemistry,
But Willie is no more.
What he took for H_2O
Was H_2SO_4.

Little Willie;
Pair of skates;
Hole in the ice;
Golden gates.

Willie in the cauldron fell;
See the grief on Mother's brow!
Mother loved her darling well;
Darling's quite hard-boiled by now.

Little Willie from the mirror licked the mercury right off,
Thinking, in his childish error, it would cure his whooping
    cough.
At the funeral Willie's mother sadly said to Mrs. Brown,
" 'Twas a chilly day for Willie when the mercury went down!"

Willie fell down the elevator—
Wasn't found till six days later.
Then the neighbors sniffed, "Gee whiz!
What a spoiled child Willie is!"

Willie on the railroad track—
The engine gave a squeal.
The engineer just took a spade
And scraped him off the wheel.

Willie, with a thirst for gore,
Nailed the baby to the door.
Mother said, with humor quaint,
"Willie, dear, don't spoil the paint."

While most of these rhymes featured Willie himself, it was permissible to bring other gruesome characters into the act.

THE WILLIES

Father nailed his darling wife
Fast against the parquet flooring.
Tho' he was loath to take her life,
He simply had to stop her snoring.

We'll never bail our brat;
No more we'll pay his fines.
He hung himself with Dad's cravat—
Blest be the tie that binds.

My darling wife was always glum.
I drowned her in a cask of rum,
And so made sure that she would stay
In better spirits night and day.

Lucy met a train.
The train met Lucy.
The track was juicy.
The juice was Lucy.

Father, I regret to state,
Cut his daughters up for bait.
We miss them when it's time to dine,
But Father's fish taste simply fine.

Oh, tell me, Mother, what is that?
It looks like strawberry jam.
Hush, hush, my child, it's only Pa
Run over by a tram.

Merry funny little Moses
Burnt off both his brothers' noses;
And it made them look so queer
Mama said: "Why, Moses dear!"

Sam had spirits naught could check,
And today, at breakfast, he
Broke his baby sister's neck,
So he shan't have jam for tea!

An angel bore dear Uncle Joe
To rest beyond the stars.
I miss him, oh! I miss him so—
He had such good cigars.

Making toast at the fireside,
Nurse fell in the fire and died.
And, what makes it ten times worse,
All the toast was burned with Nurse.

Unlike the limerick, which was the first cousin to the Little Willie (the bawdy cousin of the cruel cousin), the Little Willie has not been brought up to date. This is a shame, since there is so much to work with. A few examples begged to be written in hopes of helping to spark a revival.

Willie stole a van from Sears,
Drove it through a field of peers.
Now he said with quite a shout:
"My day-care center's all wiped out."

Willie slugged his sitter,
Broke her nose, and bit her.
Why he did is plain to see—
Too much violence on TV.

· 13 ·

Making Mary

It is axiomatic that the sweeter and the more innocent the nursery rhyme, the greater is the urge to rewrite it with the same venomous pen that gave us the vile Willie.

Here is some of what several generations of anonymous doggerelists have done to Mary, her lamb, and her contrariness.

Mary had a little watch;
She swallowed it one day.
Now she's taking Epsom salts
To pass the time away.

Mary had a kitten,
Tommy had a pup,
Alphonse had a crocodile,
Which ate the others up.

Mary had a little lamb,
Also a little bear.
I've often seen her little lamb—
My story ends right there.

Mary had a little lime
And quite a lot of gin,
And everywhere that Mary went
She didn't know she'd been.

Mary had a little lamb,
The lamb had halitosis,
And everywhere that Mary went
The people held their noses.

Mary had a little pet—
'Twas neither lamb nor gopher.
She most enjoyed her little pet
Upon the parlor sofa.

Mary had a little lamb,
But the boys gave her no tumble.
Now Mary's grown and has two calves
That make the boys all mumble.

Mary had a bathing suit,
The latest style, no doubt;
And when she got inside it she
Was more than halfway out.

Little Mary on the ice
Went with her friends to frisk.
Wasn't Mary being nice,
Her pretty * ?

MAKING MARY

Mary had a little lamb
Before she learned to think.
Now she's blond and men are fond
Of keeping her in mink.

Mary had a little swing,
It isn't hard to find,
And everywhere that Mary goes
The swing is just behind!

Mary had a little lamb,
A lobster and some prunes,
A glass of milk, a piece of pie,
And then some macaroons.
It made the naughty waiters grin
To see her order so,
And when they carried Mary out
Her face was white as snow.

Mary had a little lamb,
Its feet were black as soot,
And everywhere that Mary went
His sooty foot he put.

Mistress Mary, quite contrary,
Just lets her mustache grow—
"Why should I take such pains," she says,
"To please the average Joe?"

Mary, Mary quite contrary,
What does your garden grow?
"Silver bells and cockleshells
And one damn petunia."

· 14 ·

Punishments

o collection of puns would be complete without a collection of these:

A

Acoustic: Instrument used in billiards.
Advice: Massage parlor commercial.
Alarms: Describing an octopus.
Ascend: [Most people know what this is without definition.]
Aseptic: Doubter with a cold.
Aspire: How Cleopatra died.
Asterisk: Hazard in space.
Austere: Source of au jus.
Autopsy: Roof of a car.
Aversion: One side of a disputed story.

B

Bacteria: The rear portion of a cafeteria.
Bandeau: Forbidden French water.
Bar Stool: What Davy Crockett stepped in.
Becon: Meat from the sides of a hog.
Bewitches: I'll be right there soon.
Bigamist: Fog in Italy.
Bigamy: Large pygmy.
Bullion: Mythical beast, half bull, half lion.
Buoyant: Male insect.

C

Camelot: Where humped beasts are parked.
Candle: Jarred pickles?
Candor: Opening to the john.
Cantilever: State of male monogamy.
Casualty: Informal British repast.
Category: Cat run over by steamroller; also long puss.
Cede: To have seen.
Cello: German Jell-O.
Cherub: Furniture polish.
Cistern: Opposite of brethren.
Cochineal: To bash a small, narrow fish.
Coincide: What you do when it starts to rain.
Collapse: How an audience reacts to a performance.
Comatose: Foot grooming.
Commentator: Undistinguished potato.
Conceit: Eye strain.
Condense: Prison prom.
Condominium: Midget's birth control device.
Cognac: What a yak puts ice cream in.
Coward: Bovine direction.

Crocodile: Jar of soap.
Cruelty: Difficult hole in golf.
Custody: Custardlike.

D

Debate: What lures de fish.
Decontrol: Ugly church officer who lives in a cave.
Denial: Egyptian river.
Despair: Tire kept for emergencies.
Dialogue: How you call a tree.
Dictum: Harry's two companions.
Digest: Morbid joke.
Dilate: To live long.
Diploma: The person who fixes the pipes.
Documentate: What you say to the doctor when he charges you ten dollars for an eight-dollar procedure.
Domineer: Cheap corn, as contrasted with *buccaneer*, expensive corn.
Dromendary: Store that sells milk to camels.
Dulcet: Inferior tennis.

E

Eclipse: What the gardner does to the hedge.
Elliptical: A kiss.
Exorbitant: A costly satellite that has fallen out of the sky.

F

Farcical: Long bike ride.
Flippant: Smart-alec termite.
Footstool: Bathroom feat.
Fulgent: Man after a large dinner.

Fungi: A comedian; the life of the party.
Furlong: The hair on a shaggy dog.

G

Gastric: Cleverness dependent on flatulence.
Geometry: What an acorn says when it is grown up.
Gherkin: Relatives with a tendency to make one growl.
Gneiss: Compliment made to metamorphic rocks.
Grimace: Ace of spades.

H

Hundred: What Attila induced.
Hypotenuse: Washroom upstairs is occupied.
Hypothesis: Opening words when a child calls home.

I

Ideal: Poker table cry.
Igloo: Eskimo toilet.
Impunity: Agreement among devils.
Incongruous: Where our laws are made.
Innuendo: Italian for Preparation H.
Insolvent: Description of a man entering a delicatessen.
Isolate: Rabbit's exclamation from *Alice in Wonderland*.

J

Jaguar: Battle involving a bunch of drunks.
Japonica: Imported vehicle.
Jonquil: Pen meant for use in rest room.

K

Kennel: Waterway.
Kimono: Japanese refusal to mow lawn.

L

Laundress: Garb for outdoor party.
Lithe: Told by bad boys.
Locale: How President Coolidge was greeted at times.
Locus: Obscene muttering.
Logarithm: Song sung in the north woods.
Lubber: Rubber in Japan.
Lugubrious: Fond of peanuts.

M

Macadam: The first Scotsman.
Marigold: Find a rich spouse.
Meretricious: Seasonal greeting, with "Happy New Year."
Metronome: Subway pixie.
Migraine: Possessive farmer talking about his wheat.
Mycologist: Loyal alumnus.

N

Nitrate: Lower than the day rate.

O

Obituary: Snake's exclamation after biting man.
Oboe: British bum.
Ohm: Englishman's castle.
Oscilloscope: Meter that often gives ridiculous readings.

P

Paradox: Medical partnership.
Pasteurize: Too far to see.
Paucity: Depressed municipality.
Politics: A parrot that has swallowed a watch.
Polygon: Dead parrot.
Preternatural: Additive-free preter.
Program: Metric advocate.
Ptarmigan: Pbird.

Q

Quadrillion: Dance requiring four million participants.
Quoit: Absolutely.

R

Raucus: Bad language.
Rheumatic: Upper apartment.

S

Scintillate: No set time for ceasing to lust.
Senile: Reason for going to Egypt.
Sewer: One who brings legal action.
Sexton: 2,000 pound lot of titillation.
Singapore: Negative feedback at La Scala.
Specimen: Italian astronaut.
Sqalid: Hat worn by Indian woman.
Staple: Irish church tower.
Stoic: Bird that brings babies.
Suburban: Liquor served on a submarine.

T

Tangent: Man returned from the beach.
Tirade: Retaliation for panty raid.
Torque: Tortured conversation.
Toupee: Dutch treat.

U

Uranium: Storm exclamation.

V

Valorus: Large animal vit tusks; lives in vater.
Variola: Ancient.
Velocity: We lost a hot drink.
Varicose veins: Veins that are very close to one another.
Violin: Bad hotel.
Viper: Found on the windshield of a European car.

W

Warehouse: Cry of person lost in blizzard.
Wino: Opposite of "Why, yes."

X

Xerophyte: No argument.

Z

Zealotry: What a tree salesman likes to do.
Zebra: The largest bra available.

· 15 ·

Many Hands Make Light Work

Light bulb jokes took off in the late 1970s, continue to multiply, and clearly exemplify that formula jokes are still an extremely hot item. Their lineage is easily traced. The first was an ethnic slur:

Q. How many ＿＿＿＿＿＿＿ does it take to screw in a light bulb?
  A. Five. One to hold the bulb and four to turn the chair.

Suddenly you heard variations everywhere, and before long they were being discussed in academic journals in terms of profound social trends: ". . . we are joking about our own potential lack of sexual and political power," said Alan Dundes in *Western Folklore,* and Judith B. Kerman used the pages of the *Journal of American Folklore* to term them a metaphor for "social action and decision making in technological times. . . ."

On a more overt level they were throwbacks, an excuse for stereotyping in an age when stereotyping wasn't acceptable.

Here is one of the largest collections in captivity carefully assembled to insult just about everybody.

Q. How many *actors* does it take to change a lightbulb?
 A. 100. One to change it and 99 to stand around and say "I could have done that."

Q. How many *Americans* . . .
 A. One.
(This one got a second lease on life immediately following Operation Desert Storm.)

Q. How many *appliance salesmen* . . .
 A. Only one, but that is this week and this week only.

Q. How many *auto mechanics* . . .
 A. Six. One to force it with a hammer and five to go out for more bulbs.

Q. How many *ayatollahs* . . .
 A. None. There were no light bulbs in the thirteenth century.

Q. How many *baby-sitters* . . .
 A. None. They don't make Pampers small enough.

Q. How many *bankers* . . .
 A. Four. One to hold the bulb and three to try to remember the combination.

Q. How many *Beverly Hills realtors* . . .
 A. Three. One to screw it in and two to learn Farsi.

Q. How many *bluegrass musicians* . . .
 A. One to screw it in and one to complain that it's electrified.

Q. How many *British Navy officers* . . .
   A. Only one, but it takes him seven weeks to get there.
(This was popular during the Falkland crisis.)

Q. How many *bureaucrats* . . .
   A. One to spot the burned-out bulb, his supervisor to au-
      thorize a requisition, a requisition typist, twelve clerks to
      file requisition copies, a mail clerk to deliver the requisi-
      tion to the purchasing department, a purchasing agent to
      order the bulb, a clerk to forward the purchasing order, a
      clerk to mail-order the bulb, a receiving clerk to receive
      the bulb . . .
   A. One to screw it in, one to screw it up.
   A. None. "We contract out for things like that."
   A. One, but he'll need two outside consultants to help.
   A. Two. One to assure us that everything possible is being
      done while the others screw the bulb into a water faucet.

Q. How many *Californians* . . .
   A. Three. One to change the bulb and two to share the ex-
      perience.
   A. Three. One to change the bulb and two to say, "Oh, wow!"
   A. None. Californians don't screw in light bulbs, they screw
      in hot tubs.

Q. How many *chiropractors* . . .
   A. Only one, but it will take at least 14 weekly visits.

Q. How many *college basketball players* . . .
   A. Only one, but he gets three credits for doing it.

Q. How many *computerists* . . .
   A. None. Real computerists only use LEDs.
(This is one of twelve answers to this question developed by
Jim Rubins of Napa, California. Most could be truly appreciated

only by computerists; e.g., "Hundreds have died trying to put a
± 5-volt device in a 110-volt peripheral slot," or "That depends
on how unreadable the documentation is.")

Q. How many *doctors* . . .
   A. That depends on whether or not it has health insurance.

Q. How many *economists* . . .
   A. At least four. The first to write a paper on the theory of
   changing light bulbs. The second to write a paper attacking
   the first paper. The third to call an electrician to do the
   job. And the fourth to write a paper ten years later criticizing
   the third's choice of electrician because the bulb burned
   out.

Q. How many *editors* . . .
   A. Two, one to change the bulb and one to issue a rejection
   slip to the old bulb.

Q. How many *European ballet troupes* . . .
   A. None. They like Danzig in the dark.

Q. How many *evolutionists* . . .
   A. Only one, but it takes him eight million years.

Q. How many *feminists* . . .
   A. "Hey! Watch it, buster!"
   A. "That isn't funny."
   A. Two. One to change the bulb and one to write about how
   it feels.

Q. How many *firemen* . . .
   A. Four. One to change the bulb and three to cut a hole in
   the roof.

Q. How many *football players* . . .
   A. One, but eleven get paid for it.

Q. How many *gay men* . . .
   A. Five. One to screw it in and four to stand back and say, "It's to die."

Q. How many *graduate students* . . .
   A. Only one, but it takes him seven years.
   A. Two, and a professor to take credit.
   A. It all depends on the size of the grant.

Q. How many *grocery store cashiers* . . .
   A. Are you kidding? They won't even change a five-dollar bill.

Q. How many *humor theorists* . . .
   A. Three hundred. One to change the bulb and 299 to analyze it to death.
(This appeared in the *Washington Post* of August 30, 1982, where it was attributed to Desmond McHale of Cork, Ireland, at the end of the Third International Conference on Humor. McHale was reacting to such topics as "The Early Development of Children's Appreciation of Disparagement Humor" and "Humor in Contemporary American and European Architecture.")

Q. How many *Iranians* . . .
   A. One hundred. One to screw it in and ninety-nine to hold the house hostage.

Q. How many *Japanese industrialists* . . .
   A. Three. One to make sure the new bulb is not foreign, one to change the bulb, and one to look into the export potential of the old bulb.

Q. How many *Jewish mothers* . . .
A. None. "It's all right, I'll just sit here in the dark."

Q. How many *jerks who ask stupid questions* . . .
A. Change it to what?

Q. How many *Kentuckians* (Nebraskans, etc.) . . .
A. What's a light bulb?

Q. How many *lawyers* . . .
A. Three: Two to argue the question of weather the bulb is permanently burned-out or is only temporarily disabled by being turned off, and the third to judge the issue, based on whether the public currently favors darkness or light.

Q. How many *liberals* . . .
A. One liberal and 28 delegates representing all the social, economic, and ethnic communities.

Q. How many *libertarians?*
A. It takes zero libertarians—the private sector will take care of it.

Q. How many *loggers* . . .
A. One, but he uses a chain saw.

Q. How many *Marin County Californians* . . .
A. Five. One to screw it in and four to sit in the hot tub and discuss the environmental impact.

Q. How many *Martians* does it take to screw *in* a light bulb?
A. Two, but they're very tiny.

Q. How many *massage parlor attendants* . . .
A. Whatever number turns you on, big boy.

Q. How many *medflies* . . .
A. None. They do it in the fruit.

Q. How many *New Yorkers* . . .
   A. "None of your damn business."
   A. Five. One to change the bulb and four to protect him from muggers.
   A. 201. One to put it in and 200 to watch it happen without trying to stop it.

Q. How many *newsmen* . . .
   A. Only one, but he'll tell everybody.

Q. How many *Pennsylvanians* . . .
   A. None. You just hold it up and it glows by itself.
(Three Mile Island. Get it?)

Q. How many *pessimists* . . .
   A. None. The old one is probably screwed in too tight.

Q. How many *poets* . . .
   A. Three. One to curse the darkness, one to light a candle, and one to change the bulb.

Q. How many *police officers* . . .
   A. Just one, but he's never around when you need him.

Q. How many *premeds* . . .
   A. Three. One to stand on the stool and screw it in and two to kick the stool out from under him.

Q. How many *procrastinators* . . .
   A. Only one, but he's got to wait until the light is better.

Q. How many *psychiatrists* . . .
   A. Only one—but the light bulb has to really *want* to change.
   A. Only one—but it will take a very long time and will be very expensive.

Q. How many *real men* . . .
A. None. Real men aren't afraid of the dark.

Q. How many *right-wing economists* . . .
A. None. They let the market do it.

Q. How many *Russians* . . .
A. That is a military secret.

Q. How many *sex therapists* . . .
A. Two. One to screw it in, and one to tell him he's screwing it in the wrong way.

Q. How many *straight San Franciscans* . . .
A. Both of them.

Q. How many *software engineers* . . .
A. None. It's a hardware problem.

Q. How many *surrealists* . . .
A. The chair.

Q. How many *Tampa Bay Buccaneers* (*Indianapolis Colts, San Francisco Giants*, etc.) . . .
A. Two. One to screw it in and the other to recover the fumble.

Q. How many *teachers* . . .
A. One if at home, but on school time, four.

Q. How many *Teamsters* . . .
A. 14. You got a problem with that?

Q. How many *terrorists* . . .
A. 20. One to do it, 19 to develop a distraction.

Q. How many *Virginians* . . .
A. Three. One to change it and two to sit around reminiscing about how good the old bulb was.

Q. How many *waiters* . . .
A. None. Even a burned-out bulb can't catch a waiter's eye.

Q. How many *WASPs* . . .
A. Two. One to call the electrician and one to mix the martinis.

Q. How many *White House aides* . . .
A. They prefer to do it in the dark.

Q. How many *Zen Buddhists* . . .
A. Two. One to screw it in and one not to screw it in.

Q. How many *Zen masters* . . .
A. The Zen master is the light bulb.

◆ ◆ ◆

The "How many . . . " formula has been modified for other purposes. Here is one from *Public Citizen* magazine:

Q. How many people does it take to clean up a hazardous waste dump?
A. 50. A tractor driver and 49 lawyers.

Here is another:

Q. How many *Californians* does it take to water a plant?
A. Two. One to pour the Perrier and one to massage the leaves.

· 16 ·

Fort Knocks—
The Master Collector

Believe it or not, the English-speaking world harbors more than a few serious knock-knock joke collectors. Charles Orr, a retired gentleman living in Healdsburg, California, claims to have the largest collection. He now has more than 131,000 of them and is creating and collecting new ones daily. Orr, who hopes to have his collection recognized by the *Guinness Book* as a world record, is a generous man who has permitted me to use some of his state-of-the-art additions here.

Knock, Knock.
  Who's there?
  Adage.
  Adage who?
  Adage where all I can do is look!

Knock, Knock
> Who's there?
> Adam.
> Adam who?
> Adam fly in my soup.

Knock, Knock
> Who's there?
> Al Bedouin.
> Al Bedouin who?
> Al Bedouin-ter like this one will be long remembered.

Knock, Knock
> Who's there?
> Alicia.
> Alicia who?
> Alicia like me a little bit, don't you?

Knock, Knock
> Who's there?
> Anita Loos.
> Anita Loos who?
> Anita Loos about 20 pounds.

Knock, Knock
> Who's there?
> Anwar.
> Anwar who?
> Anwar sorry about the rain delay!

Knock, Knock
> Who's there?
> Asimov.
> Asimov who?
> Asimov-ie it's even better.

Knock, Knock
    Who's there?
    Avery and Happy.
    Avery and Happy who?
    Avery meretricious and a Happy New Year!

Knock, Knock
    Who's there?
    Cat gut.
    Cat gut who?
    Cat gut your tongue?

Knock, Knock
    Who's there?
    Chiquita.
    Chiquita who?
    Chiquita little last night?

Knock, Knock
    Who's there?
    Censure.
    Censure who?
    Censure so smart, why aren't you rich?

Knock, Knock
    Who's there?
    Codicil.
    Codicil who?
    I've codicil-y wife.

Knock, Knock
    Who's there?
    Creature.
    Creature who?
    Creature old friend with a hug.

Knock, Knock
> Who's there?
> Darwin.
> Darwin who?
> Darwin young man on the flying trapeze.

Knock, Knock
> Who's there?
> Despair.
> Despair who?
> Despair tire is flat.

Knock, Knock
> Who's there?
> Effervescent.
> Effervescent who?
> Effervescent for wine, women, and song, he'd be a perfect husband.

Knock, Knock
> Who's there?
> Elsewhere.
> Elsewhere who?
> Elsewhere it's true!

Knock, Knock
> Who's there?
> Evita.
> Evita who?
> Evita shut up we wouldn't have gotten a ticket!

Knock, Knock
> Who's there?
> Ghana.
> Ghana who?
> Ghana wash that man right out of my hair.

Knock, Knock
  Who's there?
  Gil.
  Gil who?
  Gil the umpire!

Knock, Knock
  Who's there?
  Hair comb.
  Hair comb who?
  Hair comb the bride!

Knock, Knock
  Who's there?
  Hero.
  Hero who?
  Hero today, gone to Maui!

Knock, Knock
  Who's there?
  Hindu.
  Hindu who?
  Hindu each life a little rain must fall!

Knock, Knock
  Who's there?
  Hopi.
  Hopi who?
  Hopi quiet!

Knock, Knock
  Who's there?
  Huron.
  Huron who?
  Huron my foot.

Knock, Knock
> Who's there?
> Hussein.
> Hussein who?
> Hussein at a time like this?

Knock, Knock
> Who's there?
> Ike, Ann, Howard, Lee, Waite, Tillie, Damien, Sarah, Jane, Jed, and Mary.
> Ike, Ann, Howard, Lee, Waite, Tillie, Damien, Sarah, Jane, Jed, and Mary who?
> Ike, Ann, Howard, Lee, Waite, Tillie, Damien, Sarah, Jane, Jed, and Mary-ed.

Knock, Knock
> Who's there?
> Inouye.
> Inouye who?
> Inouye you want it, big boy!

Knock, Knock
> Who's there?
> Ivan.
> Ivan who?
> Ivan to be alone!

Knock, Knock
> Who's there?
> Wanda.
> Wanda who?
> Wanda make something out of it?

Knock, Knock
>Who's there?
>Juarez.
>Juarez who?
>Juarez hell!

Knock, Knock
>Who's there?
>Lecher.
>Lecher who?
>Lecher hair hang down.

Knock, Knock
>Who's there?
>Lilac.
>Lilac who?
>She can lilac a trooper.

Knock, Knock
>Who's there?
>Lipset.
>Lipset who?
>Lipset taste wine will never taste mine!

Knock, Knock
>Who's there?
>Ma Bell.
>Ma Bell who?
>Ma Bell is out of order—knock!

Knock, Knock
>Who's there?
>Macho.
>Macho who?
>Macho do about nothing.

Knock, Knock
> Who's there?
> Mama san.
> Mama san who?
> Mama san the warpath!

Knock, Knock
> Who's there?
> Manor.
> Manor who?
> Are you a manor a mouse?

Knock, Knock
> Who's there?
> Marcus Welby.
> Marcus Welby who?
> I Marcus Welby dead for all you care!

Knock, Knock
> Who's there?
> Nadia.
> Nadia who?
> Nadia believe me?

Knock, Knock
> Who's there?
> Ng.
> Ng who?
> It's just one little Ng after another.

Knock, Knock
> Who's there?
> Nutritious.
> Nutritious who?
> Nutritious dad would drown in Watergate.

Knock, Knock
  Who's there?
  O.A.
  O.A. who?
  O.A. down south in Dixie!

Knock, Knock
  Who's there?
  Omelette.
  Omelette who?
  Omelette smarter than I look!

Knock, Knock
  Who's there?
  Ooze.
  Ooze who?
  Ooze that knocking at my door?

Knock, Knock
  Who's there?
  Opal Lee.
  Opal Lee who?
  Opal Lees—just for me?

Knock, Knock
  Who's there?
  Osmosis.
  Osmosis who?
  Osmosis, who is you?

Knock, Knock
  Who's there?
  Ottawa.
  Ottawa who?
  Ottawa know St. Peter will let me in?

Knock, Knock
>Who's there?
>P.
>P. who?
>P.U.
>(Orr claims this is the shortest ever made.)

Knock, Knock
>Who's there?
>Raleigh.
>Raleigh who?
>Raleigh 'round the flag, boys.

Knock, Knock
>Who's there?
>Robin.
>Robin who?
>Robin Peter to pay Paul!

Knock, Knock
>Who's there?
>Rudolph.
>Rudolph who?
>Money is Rudolph all evil.

Knock, Knock
>Who's there?
>Sadie and Eloise.
>Sadie and Eloise who?
>Sadie word and I'll Eloise be your valentine.

Knock, Knock
>Who's there?
>Simi.
>Simi who?
>Come up and Simi sometime.

Knock, Knock
    Who's there?
    Synanon.
    Synanon who?
    Synanon my salary isn't easy.

Knock, Knock
    Who's there?
    Taipei.
    Taipei who?
    My blood is Taipei.

Knock, Knock
    Who's there?
    Wayne.
    Wayne who?
    Wayne drops keep falling on my head.

Knock, Knock
    Who's there?
    Zeus.
    Zeus who?
    Zeus company, three's a crowd.

· 17 ·

The Voice from the Audience

When this book was started, true scientific procedure was followed: Formulas were stated, procedures outlined, and objectives listed. But a glaring omission of a key formula was spotted by Timothy Perper, Ph.D., of Philadelphia. Quoting from Dr. Perper's communication:

> My favorite genre of formula jokes . . . The Voice from the Balcony/Audience.
>
> A recent and banal example is of the man working on the church ceiling, hidden amidst the rafters. Woman comes, starts to pray, loud and clear, and the painter decides to play a joke, and says thunderingly, *"I have heard your prayer!"* The woman turns, looks up, and says, "Not you, I want to talk to your mother!"
>
> The reason I think that is not funny is that one does not, in this formula joke, ever answer the Voice from the Balcony. It is the voice of the anonymous, faceless crowd, not taken in by nonsense, pretense, and such like. Here is a classic.

183

Seniors all assembled for their graduation from Barnard College, with their parents, etc., etc., all dressed up, etc., etc. The Dean, an older woman, is going on and on. "Body and mind both healthy [etc.], responsibility of womanhood [etc.], love is basic to family [etc.], not cast away promiscuously [etc.], young lady's responsibility to eschew promiscuous sex [rave, rant], dangers of wantonness [rr], pleasures of sex only transient [rr], unwanted pregnancy [rr], VD [rr, but euphemistically], loss of respectability, loss of femininity, loss of grace [rave, rant] . . . and for what? All cast away for naught but an hour of pleasure!"

Voice from audience: "How do you make it last an hour?"

And, perhaps, you have not heard (or not heard often) . . .

This was told to me as a classic of the early days of sex education, presumably just after Kinsey, when delicately and with trouble, U.S. colleges and universities were grudgingly first introducing the rudiments of sex education. And, of course, like all such stories, it was sworn to be true.

The instructor (male) was explaining something of the anatomy of the sexual organs. He had reached a description of the male genitalia, and was—with difficulty—trying to conquer his embarrassment in describing the testicles. "The human male's testicles," he said, "are approximately the size and shape of plover's eggs . . ." [In fact, early sex education tests said precisely that, so that part is true.]

Voice from the audience (female): "Well, now we know how large plover's eggs are."

Indeed, these are classics and Perper's work is important. Here are some other examples of the genre:

A new tenor makes his debut at the Met. He sings an aria and the applause is so overwhelming that he sings it again. They try to go on with the opera but the applause won't stop, so he is brought forward to sing it again. This goes on until he has sung it eight times.

Finally he steps forward and addresses his audience: "My friends, this is too much. The honor you have bestowed on me is overwhelming and no matter what becomes of me in the future, this will have been my greatest operatic moment. However, the opera must go on and my voice is tiring, so please don't ask me to sing it again."

Voice from the balcony: "You'll sing it till you get it right!"

Preacher: ". . . and furthermore, hell is filled with cocktails, roulette wheels, and naughty chorus girls."

Voice from the rear: "O death, where is thy sting?"

Reformer: "What I want is reform—tax reform, police reform, I want temperance reform, I want social reform, I want—I want—"

Voice from the rear: "What you want is chloroform."

A professor, suspecting that his class was not paying attention, decided to lapse into doubletalk in the midst of his lecture to see if his students were awake:

"The other problems associated with durnamic smolg is resorial, remtious, and refrominating policies of pullic garbistan. As is now becoming clearer, wallage, brough tabs and, occasionally, blinger twetchel are the only possible remedies."

Voice from the rear: "Fine, but what the hell are brough tabs?"

A man comes home unexpectedly one afternoon to find his wife in a negligee and a half-smoked cigar in the ashtray.

"Where," he demanded, "did the cigar come from?"

Voice from the closet: "Tampa."

The students were slow in bringing in their four dollars for the high-school yearbook and the teacher decided to put some pressure on her class.

"Just think," she said, "twenty-five years from now you can look in this book and say, 'There's Judy Jones, she's an important lawyer today, and here's Tom Smith, who's a doctor, and here's—' "

Voice from the rear: "And here's the teacher, she's dead."

Graduation speaker: "Remember, you must have initiative and go forward in life. Remember, on every door there is a little sign that says PUSH."

Voice from the rear: "And on the other side it says PULL."

Kindergarten teacher on the first day of school: "If anyone has to go to the bathroom hold up two fingers."

Voice from the back of the room: "How will that help?"

Speaker: "A horrible thing has happened. I've just lost my wallet with $500 in it. I'll give $50 to anyone who will return it."

Voice in the rear: "I'll give $100."

Professor: "Order! Order!"

Voice from the rear: "Beer!"

When Jack Benny was 82 years old, he appeared in a concert and at one point noted, "I have a violin that was made in 1729."

Voice from the rear: "Did you buy it new?"

Professor: "I will not begin today's lecture until the room settles down."

Voice from the rear: "Go home and sleep it off."

Professor: "If I saw a man beating a donkey and stopped him from doing so, what virtue would I be showing?"

Voice from the rear: "Brotherly love."

Orator at the funeral of a noted gambler: "Ace Muldoon is not dead—he only sleeps."

Voice from the rear: "Hundred dollars says he's dead."

The high-school science teacher was going over a test and commenting on the poor answers to a particular question. "This question was designed to make you think."

Voice from the back of the room: "Trick question! Trick question!"

Muldoon's mortality suggests the voice that is heard at the last edge of life:

The children are arguing as to the number of limousines that should be in their father's funeral. The noise gets louder and the arguments more acrimonious.

Voice from the edge: "Help me up and I'll walk."

"Where should the old man be buried?" said one of the children. The question touched off a long discussion on the relative merits of a half-dozen cemeteries.

Voice from the edge: "Surprise me!"

The voice from the rear naturally leads to the issue of hecklers—voices from the audience gone out of control. There have been hundreds of great one-liners used to neutralize those voices that can't be stilled with a mere request to be quiet. Here are some of the better examples used over the years by platform speakers and performers:

Sir, if they ever put a price on your head, take it.

This man's not himself today—and it's a great improvement.

You're snappy on the comeback—just like your checks.

Please don't talk while I'm interrupting.

There, ladies and gentlemen, is the greatest argument yet advanced for twin beds.

Lady, you wouldn't like it if I came to the place where you worked and turned out the red light.

Sir, you have more nerve than an abscessed tooth.

When I was a kid on the farm I accidentally killed our donkey with an ax, and my father told me that someday that jackass would come back to haunt me.

Sir, if Moses had seen you, there would have been another commandment.

Would you mind sitting down, sir? The funny suit contest isn't until later.

Look! The face on the barroom floor just got up.

He loves nature in spite of what it did to him.

Why not give me a call later—and I can hang up on you.

That man's always got a chip on his shoulder—his head.

Would you take something downstairs for me? The elevator.

I came in here with a terrible headache—but compared to you it's a pleasure.

· 18 ·

Tourist Tips

With every newspaper and radio station now giving us all sorts of well-meaning, unsolicited advice on everything from the prevention of poinsettia fungus to wok care, there is something devilishly appealing about intentionally bad advice.

My favorite form is misleading tips for tourists. The tradition was started by the British magazine *New Statesman*, which began asking for wrongheaded tourist advice as London began filling with visitors after World War II. "Visitors in London hotels," wrote one reader, "are expected by the management to hang the bedlinen out of the windows to air." Another suggested, "If you take a taxi, the driver will be only too willing to give your shoes a polish while waiting at the traffic lights."

Inspired by the London example, I developed a list for Washington, D.C.

1. Good-natured heckling from the visitors' gallery of the Senate is a custom as old as the Republic.

2. Try the magnificent echo in the main reading room of the Library of Congress.

3. Wednesday is picture day at the Supreme Court. Pose with the robed judges. Bring the kids.

4. Washington's reputation as "The City of Singing Bus Drivers" is well deserved. Ask and you shall hear.

5. First-time riders on the new Metro subway system are, of course, expected to shake hands with all the passengers in their car on boarding.

6. A little-known 1977 reform act provides that all American citizens have access to the previously private rooms and special services of Congress.

7. One of the Treasury secretary's greatest pleasures comes from personally redeeming matured savings bonds. Appointment suggested, but not required.

8. Prostitution is under firm control in the District of Columbia. Most work only in daylight and can be found in and around federal buildings. They can be identified by the plastic ID cards hanging from their necks.

9. Washington's status as an international city is reflected in many ways, including the playful Oriental bazaar at our better stores. In other words, haggling is the order of the day, and if you pay the asking price for an item you will immediately be marked as a rube.

10. Save an afternoon for the Interstate Commerce Commission even if you must pass up the vastly overrated and crowded White House and FBI tours.

11. Call us old fashioned, but our career women still like to be called "girls" even if the gal in question is a member of the Cabinet.

12. Most embassies expect party crashers. ("How else can we get to know 'the people'?" reasons an ambassador from a European nation.)

13. An archaic—but vigorously enforced—law still on the books from the time of the Civil War requires bar patrons to rise after each drink and assert their sobriety and allegiance to the Union.

14. You can still "do" Washington on $15 a day, but only if you confine your eating to restaurants with French-sounding names.

After this list of tourists tips appeared in *The Washingtonian* magazine, several other writers were inspired to create their own, including William D. Tammeus of the *Kansas City Star*, who came up with some useful ideas for his area:

1. Everyone in Kansas City loves and knows all the words to "Everything's Up to Date in Kansas City." Local residents consider it a breach of etiquette if you don't ask them to sing it while you're here.

2. Almost nothing is more fun than going to the stockyards and chatting with the cowboys. They're especially friendly to folks who bring along a little Red Man to chew and share.

3. Visitors who stop by Hallmark Cards are given enough greeting cards to send back home.

4. Small English towns are famous for inexpensive "bed and board" homes for travelers. Bed and board at quite reasonable rates are also available in the Kansas City area. Homes that participate are located exclusively along Ward Parkway, from the Plaza south to Gregory, and in Mission Hills. Just knock on the doors.

5. Sundays are slow news days, so the last ten or twenty minutes of local TV newscasts are reserved for tourists and conventioneers who want to drop by the studios and say "Hi!" to people out there in television land.

6. The custom of bringing your own instruments and joining in performances of the Kansas City Philharmonic is an old one. The more kazoos and tubas, the better.

7. All major hotels here expect you merely to drop off the key at the desk when you check out. They'll bill you later. "It's our way of saying 'Howdy, friend,' " says one manager.

8. Postcards featuring scenic views of Kansas City, found in nearly any drugstore, are free. Don't even bother to ask.

The possibilities are endless. Here are a few concocted with help from Robert Skole and Robert Yoakum.

Athens

Athenians are very sensitive about the condition of the ruins in and around their city. Do *not* mention them. If the Greeks themselves bring up the subject, say something consoling about urban renewal.

Bonn

Don't be obsessed with punctuality. Lateness is not only common, but preferred.

This may be the only capital city in the world where members of the parliament make morning wake-up calls for hotel guests. Just leave your name, hotel, and the time you wish to be awakened with any uniformed police officer.

Chicago

Residents of this fine place never seem to tire of being told that theirs is America's Second City. No compliment to the city should be made without prefacing the remark with "I know it is not as good as New York, but. . . ." Also, you haven't been to Chicago unless you've complained—whined is better—about the wind.

Copenhagen

On occasion, an unscrupulous restaurant owner will try to sell a vistor a sandwich without a top. Should this unpardonable offense be committed against you, stand up and at the top of your lungs shout that you will not be fooled and if the owner does not come out immediately with the sandwich tops and an apology, you will report him to the food ombudsman. The other diners will applaud.

Dallas

Residents of this city never tire of talking about the television show that bore its name for so many years. Bring up hot topics like J.R.'s true personality and the tortured history of Ewing oil, and you will be invited to all the best parties.

Chili parlors throughout the city tend to offer mild versions of this dish. When entering one of these places, announce that you understand that their chili is flavored like infant's pablum and you want the "real" stuff.

Always refer to the place as "Big D."

Edinborough

Yes, your average Scotchman (never Scot or Scotsman) loves to be ribbed about his kilt, especially by other men. If you encounter an especially large and brawny gent in a kilt, ask him for a dance.

Geneva

Ask your cab driver to swing by the magnificent nineteenth-century headquarters of the Swiss Navy. It is adjacent to the main drilling plant that puts the holes in Swiss cheese. Stop to pick up a free bag of cheese holes.

If offered fondu, mention that you got a fondu pot for a wedding present, but sold it years ago at a garage sale with all your old nondigital watches.

Hong Kong

It is a well-known fact that truck drivers always know the best places to eat. So flag down any truck, and the driver will be glad to tell you where the best Chinese restaurant is.

Lisbon

If somebody smiles at you on the street, step on the person's feet. It's a Portugese greeting.

London

The British have taken their problems with the pound in characteristic good humor. Joke about the British "funny money," and you will make friends wherever you go ... and pack a jeweler's loupe with which to examine the Crown Jewels.

Ignore all signs prohibiting parking. These are here to make sure that tourists have plenty of parking space.

Los Angeles

Hollywood studios are always looking for new movie stars. Just show up at the main gate of any of the major studios any time before noon and say that you're there for a free screen test.

Don't forget to take a leisurely walking tour along at least part of this city's freeway system. Bring a picnic lunch.

Mexico City

Hire a guide, nickname him Pancho Villa, and head off to the nearest Taco Bell to plan your itinerary.

Unlike their Northern neighbors, hotel and restaurant workers in Mexico will be insulted if you try to tip them.

New York

Pay no attention to the signs at the United Nations that say "Delegates Only." If the country you are from is a member, you are considered a delegate-at-large while in New York.

It is customary here to kiss hotel employees of the opposite sex upon checking out in lieu of a tip. The better the service, the more passionate the kiss. For employees of the same sex, a vigorous slap on the back will do fine.

The guards at Grant's Tomb never seem to tire of being asked who is buried there.

Oslo

Don't bother to pay for gasoline if you drive here. Norway's way of bragging to the world about its offshore oil is to give free fill ups to foreigners. Pay no attention to the screaming service station attendents as you pull away from the pump—it is their quaint Nordic way of saying Welcome.

Paris

Generally speaking, no native ever pays the "asking" price printed on the menus at the better restaurants in this city. Begin bargaining as soon as you get your bill and don't pay until it is at least half what is asked for. The more stars attached to a restaurant, the more they like to haggle over the bill.

Tourists who imitate Maurice Chevalier tend to get better treatment from the locals, who, incidentally, never tire of talking about Jerry Lewis with Americans.

Rome

When in Rome . . . for starters, if you get a hotel room with a balcony use it to impersonate Mussolini. If the appreciative crowd calls for an encore, do the Pope.

San Francisco

Never say San Francisco when you are here. It's "Frisco," and order Rice-a-Roni, the San Francisco treat, at any and all restaurants.

Citizens of this city are embarrassed by their ancient cable cars and are quick to agree with visitors who suggest that they be replaced with a fleet of modern buses.

Stockholm

Swedes just love being told that theirs is just one big moody, angst-ridden, Bergmanesque nation. Begin discussions about the nation's high suicide rate.

Tokyo

Waiters love to show their graciousness here. Send back your sushi and tell them you want it well done and note how pleased they are to oblige.

Practical jokes are the rage here. Ask your hotel bellman to page Leonard L. LLewellyn, sign all important contracts with a trick leaky pen, and don't forget to pack some squirting lapel flowers, exploding cigars, and whoopie cushions for business meetings.

Boast loudly about American quality control and technological uniqueness.

Toronto

Canadians never tire of being told how much they are like Americans and that—except for the weaker dollar here—Toronto is "more American" than most American cities.

If you get to a hockey game, it is the custom to yell horrible, obscene insults at the players. Watch them smile back.

Zurich

Bankers here not only like to be called "Gnomes," but love nothing more than to open secret numbered bank accounts for each member of the family, even the kids. There are no minimums, so you can all have souvenir bank accounts for less than the price of a bus ride. Check every few hours to see how much interest you've earned.

◆ ◆ ◆

It can only be hoped that this inspires more good advice, which, of course, should be written down, copied, and placed in guest bedrooms and hotel rooms.

Another fertile field for advice is energy saving. Don Addis, who illustrated this book, has come up with these fine bits of advice: ". . . put a cork in unused light sockets, use less alacrity, let your alarm clock coast, put a brick in your air conditioner, unplug the electoral college, turn off your spouse when not in use, set your microwave on 'stun,' set your blender on 'off' and your can opener at thirty-three and a third, organize a block blackout, push your riding mower, and join a moped pool. To show your support, turn off all your lights all night."

· 19 ·

Slurred Visions

For those who hold to the premise that the best offense is a good offensive joke, here are the four major categories, collected and sorted for handy aggression.

Mibbies

Slurring is a popular and long-established avocation among college students and grads. In Texas they are told about Texas A&M and are called Aggie jokes.* They tell them about Georgia Tech at the University of Georgia and about the University of Georgia at Georgia Tech and so forth. The best are Mibbie jokes, which

---

* At Texas A&M they tell Teasip jokes; the name refers to University of Texas students. A current example: An Aggie grad is forced to rent an outhouse because nobody will rent an Aggie an apartment in Austin. His mother comes to visit him and says, "How can you live like this?" The grad answers, "There are worse places to live than this. Hell, I just sublet the basement to a Teasip."

are told about the dumb-as-a-post students and alumni of Marble State.

The Mibbie football team—nicknamed the Blockheads—no longer gets ice water. The player with the recipe graduated.

Then there was the Mibbie who lost $40 on a televised college football game. He dropped $20 on the game and another $20 on the replay.

Did you hear about the Mibbie who locked his keys in the car?
It took him nine hours to get his family out.

Why did the Mibbie move his house five feet from its old foundation?
Because there was slack in his clothesline.

Did you hear about the Mibbie who cut correspondence school?
He sent in empty envelopes.

Then there was the Mibbie who threw himself on the floor and missed, and was so stupid that other Mibbies noticed.

Mibbie: "I just got a bicycle for my girlfriend."
Second Mibbie: "How did you get such a good trade?"

Did you hear about the Mibbie who, when he heard his wife was going to have twins, went out looking for the other guy?

One day a Mibbie came home to find his wife in bed with an Aggie. In a fit of grief, the Mibbie took out a gun and placed it to his temple.
The Aggie, feeling remorseful, said, "Hey, buddy, don't feel so upset . . . this kind of thing happens all the time. Have a beer and forget it."

The Mibbie, with the gun still at his head said, "Shut up, stupid . . . *you're next!*"

Then there was a Mibbie whose wife asked him to change the baby. He showed up an hour or so later with another child. But he was to be pitied: According to what his friends say, this Mibbie's wife had legs so hairy her knees had bangs. And when she cooked, she tended to burn the meat so badly they had to check dental records to see what they were eating.

Did you hear about the Mibbie who willed his body to science?
Science is contesting the will.

Did you hear about the four Mibbies in a pickup truck that went into a canal? The two in the front were saved, but the two in back were lost because the tailgate was stuck.

Then there was a Mibbie who put on one boot because the weather forecaster called for only one foot of snow.

"Don't you ever peel the banana before eating it?" said the man to the Mibbie.
"No. I already know what's inside."

Then there was the Mibbie football star who, when he got his varsity letter, had to have his girlfriend read it to him.

How many Mibbies does it take to eat a rabbit dinner?
Three. One to feast, and two to watch in each direction for cars.

Then there was the Mibbie who tried to have his marriage annulled when he found out her father had no license for the gun.

A Mibbie first smells his right armpit and smiles, then smells his left and frowns. "What's going on?" says a passerby. The Mibbie replies, "They haven't invented Left Guard yet."

Then there was the absentminded Mibbie professor who forgot to write a $25 introductory text to sell his students.

Then there was the Mibbie who tried to trade his wife's menstrual cycle in on a new Honda.

Two Mibbies were building a house. One, examining each nail as he picked it up, was tossing about half of them away.
"What's the matter?" asked the second Mibbie.
"About half of these nails have the head on the wrong end."
"You fool, those are for the other side of the house."

Funistradans

Ethnic insult jokes are perennial and, over time, tend to become omnidirectional. What is a Polish joke in Chicago is a Norwegian joke in Minneapolis, a "Newfie" joke in Toronto, a Tasmanian joke in Canberra, and an Irish joke in Boston. One group that has not gotten equal time are the witless Funistradans.* Their time has come.

How much does a Funistradan pay for a haircut?
Four dollars—a buck for each side.

What do you call a man walking around with his hands in the air?
A Funistradan on war maneuvers.

Why are Funistradan mothers so strong?
It comes from raising dumbbells.

---

* Psychologist Jeffrey H. Goldstein argued in *Human Behavior* magazine that this kind of joke loses its punch if a fictitious nationality is used. The example he used were East Frisians. For this very reason I have shied away from a silly, fictitious nationality and will take my lumps for maligning Funistradans. If you have trouble finding it in your atlas, it is right next to Galubria.

What's this? (Asked with one's arms folded across one's chest.)
A Funistradan bra.

Do you know the difference between a Funistradan wedding and a Funistradan funeral?
There's one less drunk at a Funistradan funeral.

Why do flies have wings?
To beat Funistradans to the garbage cans.

What is a group of Funistradan paratroopers called?
Air pollution.

Who shot Mussolini eight times?
Five hundred Funistradan sharpshooters.

How do Funistradans propose?
You're going to have a *what*?

What has an IQ of 192?
Funistrada.

How can you spot a Funistradan airplane?
It has hair under its wings.

How do you get a one-armed Funistradan out of a tree?
Wave.

Why aren't Funistradans allowed to play bingo?
They eat the corn.

What are 20 Funistradans lying on a lawn?
Fertilizer.

What's the easiest job in the world?
The head of Funistradan Intelligence.

What is gross stupidity?
One hundred forty-four Funistradans.

What do you have when you extend your little finger?
A Funistradan handkerchief.

What did the Funistradan do when he won an Olympic gold medal?
He had it bronzed.

Do you know why Funistradans get only half an hour off for lunch?
If they had an hour, they'd have to be retrained.

How does a Funistradan grease his car?
He runs over a Galubrian.

How does a Funistradan fan himself?
Holds his hand still and waves his face in front of it.

Why is Santa Claus Funistradan?
Who else would wear a red suit during the holidays?

Why don't they let Funistradans operate elevators?
They forget the route.

How many Funistradans does it require to take a picture off the wall?
Ten. One to hold the picture and nine to knock down the wall.

How can you tell where a rich flamingo lives?
By the wrought-iron Funistradans on the front lawn.

What happened when the Funistradan put snow tires on his car?
They melted.

How can you tell when a Funistradan has passed away?
The garbage trucks go around with their lights on.

What does it say on the bottom of Coke bottles in Funistrada?
  Open other end.

How does a Funistradan spell *farm*?
  Ei-yi-ei-yi-o.

How do you make a Funistradan shish kebab?
  Shoot an arrow into a garbage can.

Why does one occasionally see Funistradans pushing a house down the street?
  That's how they jump-start their furnaces.

What do you do when a Funistradan throws a hand grenade at you?
  You pull out the pin and throw it back.

Why don't Funistradan mothers nurse their babies?
  It hurts too much to boil their nipples.

Why do Funistradans have scratched faces on Monday morning?
  Because they eat with knives and forks over the weekend.

Why are Funistradan jokes so simple?
  So the Galubrians can understand them.

What is green, red, orange, chartreuse, purple, brown, pink, and covered with polka dots?
  A Funistradan woman dressed up for church.

What would happen if all the Funistradans in Chicago jumped into Lake Michigan?
  Lake Michigan would end up with a ring around it.

What constitutes a traditional Funistradan seven-course dinner?
  A can of sardines and a six-pack.

What is the favorite dish of Funistradan gourmets?
Pork tartare.

Why do the Funistradans have cabbage and the Arabs oil?
The Funistradans had first choice.

What is the smallest building in all of Funistrada?
The Hall of Fame.

How did the prime minister of Funistrada deal with the problem of Red China?
He bought a pink tablecloth.

Did you hear about the border dispute between the Funistradans and the Galubrians?
The Funistradans are throwing sticks of dynamite across the border, and the Galubrians are lighting them and throwing them back.

If a Funistradan and a Galubrian jumped off a 40-story building, who would land first?
The Galubrian because the Funistradan had to stop and ask directions.

How do Funistradan fishermen count their catch?
One fish . . . two fish . . . another fish . . . another fish . . . another fish.

How does a Funistradan admiral review his fleet?
Through a glass-bottomed boat.

Why did the Funistradan take a necktie back to the store?
Because it was too tight.

How does the account of a Funistradan wedding party begin?
Among the injured were . . .

Did you hear about the Funistradan grandmother who had her tubes tied?

She didn't want to have any more grandchildren.

Why do Funistradans stand up and smile when there is lightning?

They think their pictures are being taken.

Did you hear about the Funistradan national lottery?

You can win a dollar a year for a million years.

Did you hear about the Funistradan terrorist who was unable to blow up a bus?

He kept burning his lips on the tailpipe.

One Funistradan meets another on a road and notices that he has a bag of fried chicken. "Can I have some?" he asks.

"Why should I give you any?"

"Okay. If I can guess how many chickens you have in the sack, could I have some?"

"If you can guess how many chickens are in here," says the second man, "you can have both of them."

"Three," says the first man.

A Funistradan, a Swede, and an Italian were passing a particularly smelly pigsty and decided to have a contest to see who could stay in the sty the longest. After five minutes the Italian came out, after ten the Swede came out, and after twenty minutes the pigs came out.

State of the Art

This war broke out in the early 1980s, and the biggest conflicts were reported regularly. "Insults and bitter barbs are the ammunition of the Great Midwestern Joke War now raging between

Iowa and Minnesota," said the *Los Angeles Times* in late 1982, while *USA Today* proclaimed that it was breaking out wherever there is "any kind of regional identity." These examples were carefully collected to insult the residents of at least half the states:

Who has a beard, wears a dirty white robe, and rides a pig?
Lawrence of Arkansas.

Why is it impossible to walk across New Jersey?
Nobody can hold his nose for that long.

Why are there no active volcanoes in California?
There are no virgins to sacrifice.

What is progress in Florida?
Separate electric chairs for smokers and nonsmokers.

What do they call an Oklahoman with indoor plumbing?
Kinky.

What's the difference between North Dakota and yogurt?
Yogurt has culture.

What do they call a handsome, intelligent man in New Hampshire?
A tourist.

What is the trendy new drink in South Dakota?
Perrier and water.

What do they call anyone with an IQ of 90 in Louisiana?
Governor.

Did you hear about the Iowan who was killed in a pie-eating contest?
The cow sat on him.

Did you hear that they had to close down the Georgia State Library?
Somebody stole the book.

What do they call the alphabet in Indiana?
The impossible dream.

What is the last thing a Kansas stripper takes off?
Her bowling shoes.

What do they say in Tennessee when a manure silo falls over?
Shoot the looters.

What do they call a 1954 Buick in Alabama?
The bridal suite.

What do you call two dirty teddy bears and a tractor that won't start?
The Maine State Fair.

What do you call a place with ten thousand lakes, five thousand swamps, and one fish?
Minnesota.

How did the man from Wisconsin break his arm raking leaves?
He fell out of the tree.

Why did they have to remove the speed bumps from the roads in Kentucky?
People were doing their laundry on them.

What's the most popular television show in Montana?
"90 Minutes"—they have to slow the show down so people can follow it.

Why do New Mexicans drink less Kool-Aid than folks in other states?
> Because they have such a hard time getting two quarts of water into that little envelope.

What is inscribed on beer bottles sold in West Virgina?
> Open other end.

Why do they have artificial turf at the University of Nebraska stadium?
> So the cheerleaders won't graze at halftime.

How does a Texan tell the milkman he wants extra cottage cheese?
> He pins a note to his wife's bra.

What do they call a person with shoes in South Carolina?
> A yuppie.

♪　　　♪　　　♪　　　♪

Take That

One of the oldest forms of personal insult is the kind that turns on the word *that*.* Here is an introductory selection:

He was so vain that he had his X rays retouched.
Her life was so dull that she looked forward to dental appointments.
He was so mean that he enjoyed reading Horatio Alger books backwards.
She was so dumb that she thought a buttress was a female goat.
He was so dull that his dog got bored and left him.

---

* Lest there be any confusion, *that* jokes are applied not only to individuals; for instance, "It was so cold in Chicago that I saw an alderman with his hands in his own pocket," or "This town was so small that the town slut was a virgin."

Her luck was so bad that her contacts got cataracts.

He was so dumb that he couldn't tell you which way an elevator was going if you gave him three guesses.

She was so bowlegged and he was so knock-kneed that when they stood together they spelled *OX*.

He was so nervous that he kept coffee awake.

She was so ugly that when she walked into a room the mice jumped on a chair.

His feet were so big that he had to put his pants on over his head.

She was so cheap that she only did crossword puzzles vertically so that she wouldn't have to come across.

He was so lazy that he married a pregnant woman.

He was so rich that the Joneses try to keep up with him.

She had such bony legs that when she sat down, her knees made a fist.

He was so dumb that when he rented a room the landlady left the VACANT sign up.

She was so thin that when she wore a fur coat she looked like a pipe cleaner.

He was so thin that when he closed one eye he could pass for a needle.

She had been married so many times that she had rice marks on her face.

He was so dumb that he had to ask his wife to take her sweater off to count to two.

She was so unattractive that she had to get BO to attract attention.

She was so rich that she sent her dishes out to be dry-cleaned.

He was so cheap that he ate beans to save money on bubble bath.

Her nose was so upturned that every time she sneezed, she blew her hat off.

He was so fat that he had to make two trips when he left the house.

She spent so much time in parked cars that they are now showing her on some road maps.

He was so dumb he thought a Band-Aid was a charitable organization for musicians.

She was so cheap that she used only one ice cube when she had a headache.

He was so cheap that he wouldn't even tip in a canoe.

She had so many double chins that she could wear a string of pearls without the string.

He was so slow that they had to show him how the wastebasket worked the first day on his new job.

She was so dumb that she thought the Pied Piper was a drunken plumber.

He was so self-conscious that when he went to a football game and the players went into a huddle, he thought they were talking about him.

She was so thin that when she swallowed an olive three men left town.

He was so cross-eyed that when he cried, the tears from his left eye landed on his right cheek.

She was so ugly that when she was a child her parents always took her along so that they wouldn't have to say good-bye.

He was so fat that he could only play seek.

She was so dumb that she thought you had to take music lessons to fiddle around.

He was so dumb that the fortune-teller read his mind for half price.

She was so dumb that she thought Alexander Haig was a drink made of Scotch and milk.

His breath was so bad that they pushed him over three times last Halloween.

She was so dumb that she thought *Forever Amber* was a stalled traffic light.

He was so dumb that he thought Einstein was one beer.

She was so dumb that she thought Eartha Kitt was an Italian gardening set.

SLURRED VISIONS

His nose was so big that he could smoke a cigar in the shower.

She was such a prude that she blushed when someone said "intersection."

He was so crooked that he could stand in the shadow of a corkscrew.

She was so cross-eyed that she thought the sun set in the east.

He was so crooked that when he pulled the wool over your eyes it was 50 percent polyester.

She was so dumb that when she saw a sign that said MURDERER WANTED she applied for the job.

He was so cheap that he died of oneberculosis.

It was so cold in Chicago last week that a flasher walked up to a woman and described himself.

· 20 ·

Eternal Questions

Undoubtedly there are other answers to these questions, but there are limits.

"Who was that lady I saw you with last night?"
  "That was no lady, that was my wife."

"Who was that lady I saw you with last night?"
  "That was no lady, that was your wife."

"Who was that lady I saw you with last night?"
  "That was no lady, that was my wife."
"Don't be silly. *I'm your wife.*"

"Who was that lady I saw you out with last night?"
  "I wasn't out, I was just dozing."

ETERNAL QUESTIONS

"Who was that lady I seen you with last night?"
  "You mean, 'I saw.' "
"Okay—who was that eyesore I seen you with last night?"

"Who was that lady I saw you with last night?"
  "That was no lady, that was a grapefruit—when I squeezed her, she hit me in the eye."

"Who was that lady I saw you out wit' last night?"
  "Who said I could outwit a lady?"

Lancelot to Guinevere: "Who was that last knight I saw you out with, Lady?"

Cain: "Who was that lady I saw you out with last night?"
  Adam: "That wasn't night, that was Eve."

First cannibal: "Who was that lady I saw you with last night?"
  Second cannibal: "That was no lady, that was my lunch."

"Who was that gentleman I saw you with last night?"
  "That was no gentleman, that was a senator."

"Who was that wench I saw you with last night?"
  "That was no wench, that was my hammer."

Magician to woman assistant:
"Who was that lady I sawed you with last night?"
  "That was no lady, that was my half-sister."

"Why did the chicken cross the road?"
  "To get to the other side."

"Why did the chicken cross the road?"
    "Because it was a fowl proceeding."

"Why does the chicken step over the wheel rut?"
    "Because it's too far to walk around."

"Why did the hen stop in the middle of the road?"
    "She wanted to lay it on the line."

"Why didn't the elephant cross the road?"
    "He didn't want to be mistaken for a chicken."

"Why did the otter cross the road?"
    "He didn't want to be mistaken for a chicken."

"Why did the unwashed chicken cross the road twice?"
    "Because it was a dirty double-crosser."

"Why did the chicken cross the road?"
    "To get Social Security."
(You don't get it? Well, neither did the chicken; she wasn't 65.)

"Why did the cow cross the road?"
    "Because it was the chicken's day off."

"Why don't you ever see chickens in the zoo?"
    "Because they can't afford the admission."

Have you ever seen a horse fly?
    No.
Have you ever seen:
    An egg box?
    A uniform smile?

A stone step?
A board walk?
A ball park?
A key punch?
A hot dog stand?
A shoe box?
A square dance?
A picket fence?
A ginger snap?
A fire fly?
A king fish?
A home run?
A salad bowl?
A tree bark?
A hog bristle?

What do you get when you cross . . .

. . . a lion and a parrot?
I don't know, but when it talks you'd better listen.

. . . a cat with a lemon?
A sour puss.

. . . a turtle and a cow?
A turtleneck jersey.

. . . a bumblebee with a doorbell?
A hum dinger.

. . . a pig and a billy goat?
A crashing boar.

. . . a stripteaser with a tropical fruit?
A self-peeling banana.

. . . an eel and a jellyfish?
Currant jelly.

. . . a kangaroo and a raccoon?
A fur coat with pockets.

. . . a zebra and a whale?
A traffic jam.

. . . an owl and a goat?
A hootennany.

. . . an elephant with a jar of peanut butter?
You either get peanut butter with a wonderful memory or an
elephant that sticks to the roof of your mouth.

. . . a pig, a pool table, and a tall tree?
A pork-cue-pine.

. . . a chicken with a waitress?
A chicken that lays tables.

. . . a fish and an elephant?
Swimming trunks.

. . . a centipede and a turkey?
Drumsticks for everyone.

. . . a cat and a ball of wool?
Mittens.

. . . poison ivy and a four-leaf clover?
A rash of good luck.

. . . a crocodile and an abalone?
A crock-abalone.

. . . Umberto Eco and a Mafia don?
An offer you can't understand.

. . . a porcuine with a sheep?
An animal that knits its own sweaters.

. . . a sheep with a kangaroo?
A woolen jumper.

. . . a pile of hay and a vampire?
A bale o'Lugosi.

. . . a boa constrictor and pasta?
Spaghetti that winds itself around the fork.

. . . an elephant and a kangaroo?
Potholes all over Australia

. . . James Dean and Ronald Reagan?
Rebel without a clue.

. . . a stripper and a vegetarian?
A woman who doesn't want dressing on her salad.

. . . a gorilla and a mink?
A fur coat . . . but with sleeves that are too long.

. . . a flea with a rabbit?
A bug's bunny.

. . . a hen with a banjo?
A self-plucking chicken.

. . . a dentist, a manicurist, and a soldier?
Someone who fights tooth and nail.

. . . a manicurist and a chiropodist?
Someone who waits on you hand and foot.

. . . fifty thousand pigth and fifty thousand deerth?
One hundred thows and buckth.

. . . an undertaker and a snake charmer?
Don't know, but it has hiss and hearse towels.

. . . a hippo and a goose?
Something that honks before it runs you over.

. . . a psychiatrist and a sailboat?
A Freudian sloop.

. . . a shark and a parrot?
An animal that will talk your ear off.

. . . an oyster with an owl?
Pearls of wisdom.

. . . a goat and an eel?
An electric can opener.

. . . a dog and a chicken?
A pooched egg.

. . . the side of your head with an angry little girl?
Surly Temple.

What has four legs and flies?
    A picnic table.
    A dead horse.
    Two pairs of pants.

· 21 ·

Giving Them the Business

A 90-year-old investor is having lunch with his broker. "Have I got a winner for you," says the broker. "I have a stock that will triple in value in three years."

"Three years?" says the old man. "At my age I don't even buy ripe bananas."

A businessman is dying, and the priest has not yet arrived to hear his confession. The only person with him is his long-time partner. Suddenly the dying man bolts up in bed and says:

"Phil, I must confess to someone. I stole hundreds of thousands from the business, told your wife every time you even looked at another woman, and secretly sold off our most valuable patents."

His partner lowers him to the pillow and whispers, "That's OK. That's OK. I poisoned you."

Albert Einstein finds himself in heaven and is in the process of meeting his roommates.

"How are you, Professor Einstein? My name is Al and my IQ is over 170."

"Fine," says Einstein, "that means that we will be able to discuss relativity."

"I'm Pete," says a second man, "and my IQ is 155."

"Good," says the great physicist, "that means we will be able to discuss mathematical theory."

"My name is John," says a third man, "and my IQ is 125."

Einstein says, "Very good. We will be able to talk of art and culture."

"I am honored to meet you," says the fourth man, "but my IQ is only about 70."

"That's all right," says Einstein. "Tell me, where do you think interest rates are headed?"

A man suffering from terrible headaches goes to his doctor.

"Your brain is diseased and something must be done," says the doctor.

"What can be done?"

"The only possibility is a new brain transplant technique, but the problem is that the cost of a brain is not covered by medical insurance."

"Doc, I've got some money; what'll it cost me?"

"Depends on the donor," says the doctor, "A secretary's brain will cost you about $35,000 and sales reps' brains cost closer to $50,000. On the other hand, an executive's brain will set you back close to a quarter of a million dollars."

"Wait a second," says the patient, "the difference between $35,000 and $250,000 is vast: How can you justify such an incredible discrepency?"

"Simple! The executive's brain has hardly been used."

Boss: "I'm planning a salary increase."
Employee: "Wonderful. When does it become effective?"
Boss: "As soon as you do."

Boss: "You'll find a little something extra in your pay-envelope this week."
Employee: "Wonderful. What is it?"
Boss: "A pink slip."

An elderly woman is sitting on a plane and getting increasingly nervous about the thunderstorm raging outside. She turns to a minister sitting next to her:

"Reverend, you are a man of God. Why can't you do something about this problem?"

"Lady, I'm in sales, not management."

Moses was fleeing from the Egyptians with the Israelites when he came to the Red Sea. He asked God for help and was told that there was good news and bad news.

"The good news," said the voice from on high, "is that I will part the sea so that you and your people can escape."

"And the bad news?" asked Moses.

"You will have to file the environmental impact statement."

When the May Day parade was still a big deal in Moscow, a Westerner noted a phalanx of Soviet economists marching between military units.

"Why are the economists marching in ranks with the Army?" the Westerner asked then-President Leonid I. Brezhnev.

"You'd be surprised at the damage they do," said the president.

The office manager is brought into the president's office.

"Mary, there's $50,000 missing from the safe, and you and I are the only two people who have the combination. Perhaps you'd like to say something."

"Mr. Smith, why don't we each kick in $25,000 and forget about the whole thing."

· 22 ·

Martians, Lawyers, and a Few Cannibals

Certain joke characters set up such great situations that their joke popularity is all out of proportion to reality. The stars of this chapter—the Martian, the lawyer, and the cannibal—make the point in the extreme. The Martian is fiction, and there is no firm evidence to indicate that there ever were such things as true cannibal tribes. Lawyers, on the other hand, are the exception that proves something or other.

Martians

They existed before 1957, but they got their big push in October of that year when the Soviet Union put its Sputnik I into orbit. The Space Age had begun, and a new joke fad was called for.

The first thing a Martian looks for after arriving on earth is a men's room. He finds one and, on the way out the door, notices the paper towel dispenser.

"Lady," he says, "your slip is showing."

"Are you from Mars?" he asked the green man with six arms.
"Yes."
"Are you all green with six arms?"
"Yes."
"Do you all have antennas sticking out of your head?"
"Yes."
"Do you all have little black caps on top of your head?"
"Only the orthodox."

A one-foot-tall Martian lands on earth, and the first person he encounters is a beautiful six-foot-tall woman.

"Take me to your ladder, lady: I'll see your leader later."

What did the Martian say to the tomcat?
"Take me to your litter."

. . . to the supermarket manager?

"Take me to your Liederkranz."

. . . to the forest ranger who found him in a pile of leaves?

"Rake me to your leader."

During Eisenhower's presidency, a Martian landed on the White House lawn dressed in a vicuna coat and said to the Secret Service man who came out to meet him, "Lead me to your taker."

A little green man pops out of a flying saucer on Pennsylvania Avenue, walks up to Vice President Quayle and says, "Take me to your leader."

The vice president replies, "Don't be ridiculous. I hardly know the man!"

(This has been applied to every vice president since Hubert H. Humphrey.)

Late at night two newly arrived Martians walked up Second Avenue in New York eating garbage cans.

"You know," said one, "the crusts are good, but the filling is too rich for me."

"She's not only beautiful, but she's got brains," said the Martian after seeing his first computer.

Two Martians land in Las Vegas and pass a slot machine that suddenly disgorges a load of silver dollars.

One Martian turns to the other and says, "He's foolish not to be home with a cold like that."

A Martian lands in a small town, walks into a sleazy bar, and is immediately attracted to its garish jukebox.

"What's a nice girl like you doing in a joint like this?"

The Martian scout lands his spaceship at a gas station that is closed. He walks up to the first pump and says, "I am friendly. Take me to your leader." Getting no answer, he goes to the next pump and still gets no answer. After trying all the pumps, he walks back to his spacecraft and returns to Mars.

Upon arriving home, he reports to his chief, "These earthlings are terrible. They are rude and unsociable and I couldn't get a word out of them. But, boy, are they hung!"

An earth couple is carried away to Mars by a Martian spaceship. After landing, they are told that no harm will be done to them, but that the only reason they were abducted was to study them. After a cordial day of questioning, the Martian leader says, "I think we're just about done with you, but we have one final request: Could you show us how you get your babies?"

After much self-conscious hemming and hawing, the couple decide that they should perform for the sake of interplanetary understanding.

When they have finished, the Martian leader says, "How disappointing."

"Why?" says the couple in unison.

"Because that's how we make automobiles."

"Isn't she beautiful?" said the Martian as he approached a snazzy new motor scooter. "I think I'll take her back to Mars with us."

"Watch what you're doing," his partner warned. "She may be underage."

A Martian couple walks by a hardware store, and the female stops to admire the paint cans in the window.

"I'm sorry," says the man, "your old coat will have to last you another year."

Two Martians land and first encounter a television set. They turn it on and begin to watch a western.

"This is fascinating," says the first Martian to the second, "but what I can't figure out is why the hero has a biped on his back."

A Martian noticed an apartment building covered with television aerials. "Hey, kids," he yelled, "get down from there before you hurt yourselves."

Moments after the Martian has landed on earth, a large truck passes him and drops a big box on the road.

"Lady, lady," he yells, "you dropped your purse."

A Martian lands in downtown Chicago, walks over to a traffic light, and says sympathetically, "Gee, pal, you must have had a rough night."

Reporter interviewing Martian: "Do you smoke after sex?"
Martian: "I really don't know. I've never looked."

A Martian spaceship lands in the Bronx, and the impact of landing is so great that the wheels on the craft are destroyed.

Two Martians set out to find replacement wheels and to their great relief immediately encounter a store with a large assortment of wheels in the window.

"We'll take four of those wheels in the window," says one of the Martians to the shopkeeper.

"Those aren't wheels," he says. "They're bagels. They're to eat—here, try one."

The two Martians take a few bites and then one turns to the shopkeeper and says, "They aren't bad, but they'd be a lot better with cream cheese and lox."

Several Martians disguised as humans land in New York City and head straight for a fancy restaurant for lunch.

At the end of the meal, the waiter says to them, "You guys must be Martians."

"How did you know?" asks the Martian chief.

"You're the only people who've paid cash in the last six months."

A Martian who has just landed is approached by a panhandler who says, "Can you spare a dime, mister?"

"What's a dime?" asks the Martian.

"You're right. Make it a quarter."

Lawyers

The late 1980s witnessed an explosion of lawyer jokes—most of which defamed lawyers and most of which were framed as law-yerly questions and answers:

Q. What's black and brown and looks good on a lawyer?
   A. A doberman.

Q. What is a lawyer?
   A. Someone who makes sure he gets what's coming to you.

Q. Why does Washington, D.C., have 55,000 lawyers and New Jersey the most toxic dumps?
   A. New Jersey got first choice.

Q: Why was the lawyer allowed to swim through waters infested with sharks and piranhas?
   A. Professional courtesy.

Q. What do you need when you have three lawyers up to their necks in concrete?
   A. More concrete.

Q. Why are some medical laboratories now using lawyers instead of rats?

A. A number of reasons: they breed faster, will do things that rats won't do, and their handlers don't become attached to them.

◆ ◆ ◆

The best lawyer jokes, however, are not so hard-edged:

A father and lawyer decides that it is time to explain sex and procreation to his son.

He knocks on the boy's door.

"What is it, Dad?"

"I've come to explain the alleged facts of life."

A man with a problem enters a small town to make an inquiry.

"I understand you have one of the best criminal lawyers in the nation here," he says to the man at the general store.

"Well, we're pretty sure we do, but . . ."

"But what?"

"Nobody's been able to prove it."

When the King of Siam came to America for an eye operation some years ago, his American surgeon, accustomed to setting prices somewhat by ability to pay, couldn't decide what to charge the King . . . $1,000 to be a good neighbor . . . $5,000 to match his normal fee for patients with a lot of money . . . or $10,000 to prove that the operation was worth the trip?

Someone suggested that the doctor discuss the matter with the king's American lawyer in Philadelphia. He called the lawyer, presented the problem, and was told, "The answer is simple. The King is a most honorable man. Like you, he understands value.

Just send him an invoice with no amount indicated, but add a handwritten footnote that says, 'The Honorable King can do no wrong.' "

He did exactly what the lawyer suggested and a check for $175,000 came in the mail a few days later. The surgeon was overjoyed and went on a spending spree that ended with an around the world cruise.

Upon his return, his pocketbook flattened, but happy and refreshed, he opened his mail. It was a bill from the lawyer with no amount indicated but a handwritten notation that read, "The Honorable Doctor can do no wrong."

Cannibals

"Why don't you come to my house for dinner tonight?" asked the first cannibal. "We're having my mother-in-law."

"I don't like your mother-in-law," said the second.

"All right, then just come for dessert and coffee."

Trying to prove that even cannibalism can be cured, a noted psychologist takes one of the world's most notorious cannibals and puts him through five years of intense treatment and civilized schooling at a first-rate university.

After curing him totally, the psychologist tours with the man for a year to show what has been accomplished. At the end of the year, the psychologist realizes that the man is in need of a vacation so he buys him passage on an ocean cruise.

The first day he is sitting in the dining salon and the steward asks, "Would you like to see our menu?"

"No—the passenger list."

"Yes," said the cannibal after dinner, "my wife makes good soup, but I'm sure going to miss her."

"It's like lobster," said the cannibal mother to her child on seeing her first airliner, "you only eat what's inside."

Did you hear about the cannibal student who was suspended from school for buttering up his teacher? And then there was the cannibal chief's daughter who liked boys best when they were stewed. And then there was the beatnik cannibal who ate three squares a day. Not to be forgotten was the picky cannibal who announced he was fed up with people.

"Yes," said the cannibal king, "everyone's eaten."

· 23 ·

What's the Difference?

The jokes in this chapter are really hybrids—part pun and part riddle—and are among the oldest of formulas showing up in the most ancient joke and riddle books. They invariably begin with the phrase "What's the difference between . . . " and fall into two natural groups, innocent and not so innocent. Those of the latter group usually feature only half an answer, since the second half of the answer is usually painfully obvious. For instance, "What's the difference between a cactus and a caucus?" "The pricks are on the outside of a cactus." Selection from both groups:

What's the difference between a light in a cave and a dance at an inn?

One is a taper in a cavern, the other is a caper in a tavern.

What's the difference between Christopher Columbus and the lid of a dish?

One is a discoverer, the other is a dish coverer.

What's the difference between a riddle and a man's aunt who squints?

One is a query with an answer, the other an aunt, sir, with a queer eye.

What's the difference between your granny and your granary?

One is your born kin, the other is your cornbin.

What's the difference between the crown prince, an orphan, a bald man, and a mama gorilla?

One is an heir apparent, one has ne'er a parent, one has no hair apparent, and one is a hairy parent.

What's the difference between a chess player and a man who is broke?

One watches his pawn, the other pawns his watch.

What's the difference between your last will and testament and a man who has eaten as much as he can?

One's signed and dated, the other dined and sated.

What's the difference between a tenant and the son of a widow?

The tenant has to pay rents, but the son of a widow has not two parents.

What's the difference between a summer dress in winter and an extracted molar?

One is too thin, the other tooth out.

What's the difference between an auction and seasickness?

One is the sale of effects, the other the effects of a sail.

What's the difference between last week's *Newsweek* and the brewings of Guinness and Molson?
    One is out and stale, the other's stout and ale.

What's the difference between a photocopy machine and the Hong Kong flu?
    The one makes facsimiles, the other sick families.

What's the difference between a land surveyor and an ascot?
    One is agent for property, the other a proper tie for a gent.

What's the difference between a cloud and a boy getting a spanking?
    The cloud pours with rain, the boy roars with pain.

What's the difference between an organist and a cold in the head?
    One knows the stops, the other stops the nose.

What's the difference between a barber and a woman with many children?
    One has razors to shave, the other has shavers to raise.

What's the difference between a crazy hare and a counterfeit coin?
    One is a mad bunny, the other is bad money.

What's the difference between a cat and a comma?
    The cat has claws at the end of his paws, while the comma has its pause at the end of its clause.

What's the difference between a sailor and six broken clocks?
    The sailor goes to sea, the clocks cease to go.

What's the difference between a fisherman and a lazy schoolboy?
    One baits his hook, while the other hates his book.

What's the difference between a person who tries to hit all the seagulls with a rock and the person who tries to paint all the backsides of baboons?

One tries to leave no tern unstoned, the other tries to leave no stern untoned.

What's the difference between a dog losing his hair and a man painting a small building?

One is shedding his coat, the other is coating his shed.

What's the difference between an apple and a pretty girl?

The one you squeeze to get cider, the other you get 'side 'er to squeeze.

What's the difference between a gardener, a billiard player, a precise man, and a church janitor?

The gardener minds his peas; the billiard player his cues; the precise man, his p's and q's; and the church janitor, his keys and pews.

What's the difference between Noah's ark and Joan of Arc?

Noah's ark was made of wood and Joan of Arc was maid of Orleans. And now tell me the difference between Joan of Arc and Queen Elizabeth?

Joan of Arc was a wonder, Queen Elizabeth was a Tudor.

What's the difference between a man going to the second floor and a man looking upstairs?

One is stepping upstairs, the other is staring up steps.

What's the difference between a china shop and a furniture store?

One sells tea sets, while the other sells settees.

What's the difference between a duck with one wing and one with two?

A difference of a pinion.

What's the difference between an old penny and a new dime?
  Nine cents.

What's the difference between an angry circus owner and a Roman hairdresser?
  One's a raving showman, the other is a shaving Roman.

What's the difference between a bad marksman and a constipated owl?
  A bad marksman shoots and shoots and never hits.

What's the difference between a rooster and a lawyer?
  A rooster clucks defiance.

What's the difference between a seagull and a baby?
  A seagull flits along the shore.

What's the difference between a buffalo and a bison?
  You can't wash your hands in a buffalo.

What's the difference between a eunuch and an Eskimo?
  A eunuch is a massive vassal with a passive tassel, while an Eskimo is a rigid midget with a frigid digit.

· 24 ·

A School of Heard Knocks

Here is a basic repertoire of knock-knocks guaranteed to get you through a rainy afternoon at the beach, whether it be in the company of Cub Scouts or Ph.D.'s.

So that a fairly large selection could be presented here, the first three lines have been eliminated from each knock-knock. Under normal circumstances, this is unpardonable and I promise not to do it again. Also, the reader must hereby promise never to abbreviate the spoken knock-knock ritual. To do so is to rob it of its sophistication and actually make the jokes sound silly.

Adolph who?
　　Adolph ball hit me in the head. That's why I talk like this.

Alby who?
　　Alby glad when you're dead, you rascal you.

Alfred who?
> Alfred the needle if you'll sew on the button.

Agatha who?
> Agatha feelin' you're foolin'.

Amis who?
> Amis is as good as a mile.

Amos who?
> Amos-quito bit me.

Amsterdam who?
> Amsterdam tired of these knock-knocks, I could scream.

Andy who?
> Andy bit me again.

Apollo who?
> Apollo you anywhere if you'll blow in my ear.

Ardyth who?
> Ardyth da thpeech therapy offith?

Arthur who?
> Arthur any more at home like you?

Arthur who?
> Arthur mometer is broken.

Artis who?
> Artis in the eye of the beholder.

Atch who?
> Gesundheit.

Avenue who?
> Avenue heard this knock-knock joke before?

The Avon lady who?
Your doorbell's broken.

Barcelona who?
My sister doesn't go to Barcelona.

Ben Hur who?
Ben Hur an hour and she ain't in sight.

Black Panther who?
Black Panther what I wear. What do you wear?

Butch, Jimmy, and Joe who?
Butch your arms around me, Jimmy a kiss, or I'll Joe home.

Cairo who?
Cairo the boat now?

Cameron who?
Cameron film are what you need to take pictures.

Canoe who?
Canoe come out and play?

Cargo who?
Cargo beep, beep.

Celeste who?
Celeste time I'll ask you.

Centipede who?
Centipede on the Christmas tree.

Chester who?
Chester minute and I'll see.

Cigar who?
Cigarlette fever.

Cigarette who?
    Cigarette agent.

Cigarette who?
    Cigarette life if you don't weaken.

Cirrhosis who?
    Cirrhosis red and violets are blue.

Conrad who?
    Conrad the whole book.

Curtis who?
    Curtis Interruptus.

Curtis who?
    Curtis see is contagious.

Dandelion who?
    Isn't it dandelion around all day doing nothing?

Deep who?
    Deep ends on who you were expecting.

Delores who?
    Delores be an England.

Dennis who?
    Dennis the room where I keep my books.

Descartes who?
    Don't put Descartes before the horse.

Dictaphone who?
    Dictaphone back on the receiver and stop running up my bill.

Don Giovanni who?
    Don Giovanni any ice cream today?

Doughnut who?
 Doughnut open until Christmas.

Eisenhower who?
 Eisenhower late for work.

Emerson who?
 Emerson nice shoes you've got on.

Event who?
 Event that-a-way.

Eyewash who?
 Eyewash I had a million dollars.

Flo who?
 Flo ride is good for your teeth.

Formaldehyde who?
 Formaldehyden places came the hostile Indians.

Frankie who?
 Frankie, Scarlet, I don't give a damn!

Gibbon who?
 Gibbon take if you want to get along in the world.

Gus who?
 Gus who's coming to dinner.

Hence who?
 Hence lay eggs.

Henrietta and Juliet who?
 Henrietta big dinner and got sick; Juliet the same thing, but
 she's okay.

A herd who?
> A herd you were home, so I came over!

Hewlett who?
> Hewlett the cat out of the bag?

Howard who?
> Howard you today?

Howie who?
> Fine, thanks, Howie you?

Howie who?
> Howie going to get into the movie with no money?

Gunga Din who?
> Gunga Din for free 'cause I know the usher.

Hugh who?
> Hugh who to you, too.

Hutch who?
> God bless you.

Hyman who?
> Hyman, what's new and groovy

Ira who?
> Ira member Mama.

Irish stew who?
> Irish stew in the name of the law.

Irving who?
> Irving a wonderful time, wish you were here.

Isabel who?
> Isabel necessary on a bicycle?

Jeeter who?
> Jeeter get off the pot.

Just Diane who?
> Just Diane to see you.

Kleenex who?
> Kleenex are prettier than dirty necks.

Little old lady who?
> I didn't know you could yodel.

M. 'n O. who?
> M. 'n O. gonna say.

Mandy who?
> Mandy lifeboats.

Malcolm who?
> Malcolm over to see me sometime.

Marion who?
> Marion haste, repent at leisure.

Monopoly who?
> Monopoly's bigger than your nopoly.

Moron who?
> Moron the way, see below.

Morris who?
> Morris Monday; next day's Tuesday.

Mortimer who?
> Mortimer pitied than scorned.

Nixon who?
> Nixon stones will break my bones.

Nona who?
　　Nona your business.

Norman who?
　　Norman nor beast should be out on a night like this.

Norway who?
　　There's Norway this knock-knock will work.

Oblong who?
　　Oblong Cassidy. You were expecting Roy Rogers maybe?

Oklahoma who?
　　Oklahoma wash your face.

Oliver who?
　　Oliver troubles will soon be over.

Osborn who?
　　Osborn in the state of Georgia.

Oswald who?
　　Oswald my gum.

Pecan who?
　　Pecan somebody your own size.

Polly Warner who?
　　Polly Warner cracker.

Popeye who?
　　Popeye've got to have the car tonight.

Radio who?
　　Radio not, here I come.

Sagittarius who?
　　Sagittarius State Schultz.

Salada who?
  Salada bad knock-knock jokes going around.

Sarah who?
  Sarah doctor in the house?

Sherwood who?
  Sherwood like for you to let me in.

Statue who?
  Statue in there?

Stephen who?
  Stephen my toe and I'll holler.

Sweden who?
  Sweden my tea with two lumps of sugar.

Tasmania who?
  Tasmania slip 'twixt the cup and the lip.

Thelma who?
  Thelma, Pretty Maiden, are there any more at home like you?

Thesis who?
  Thesis a recording.

Thistle who?
  Thistle make you whistle.

Tijuana who?
  Tijuana play some baseball later?

Unawares who?
  Unawares what you put on first thing each morning.

Urdu who?
  She don't, but her sister Urdu.

Urologist who?
> Urologist a bunch of nuts.

Vera who?
> Vera interesting.

Walter who?
> Walter wall carpet.

Winnie who?
> Winnie you going to think up a better joke?

Wren who?
> Wren are you coming out?

Yoda who?
> Yoda most forgettable person I ever met.

Yule who?
> Yule come on down, you hear?

Yvonne who?
> Yvonne to be alone.

Thistle who?
> Thistle be the last knock-knock joke.

· 25 ·

Menagerie a Trois

When this project began, I decided to apply one of the central organizing principles of my life: the *Tom Sawyer Whitewash Principle*. It comes from the famous incident in Mark Twain's *Adventures of Tom Sawyer* in which Tom got his pals to paint a fence by using various subterfuges and lines like, "Like it? Well, I don't see why I oughtn't to like it. Does a boy get to whitewash a fence every day?" Stated most concisely, the principle holds that if you tell enough people what fun you are having, a given number will line up for a piece of action.

In this case I let all sorts of friends, acquaintances, and people who had corresponded with me regarding my other books in on the fact that I was doing a joke book—"Does a man," I asked, "get to brew up a joke book every day?"—and I got all sorts of helpers. Some came across with a gem of a joke, while others sent a raft of them. It was not as easy as it might sound: calls at odd hours to pass along a 40-year-old traveling-salesman joke, long letters crammed with old lines from *Captain Willie's Whiz Bang* (honest!), and more.

But a handful of these stalwarts went beyond the basic notion of a few pet jokes and offered a coherent collection of original-theme jokes. Curiously, 86.2 percent of these were based on animal and vegetable themes. Here are three of these remarkable collections, which also show that it is not only possible to get help painting a fence, but that some people will build a new section of fence for you.

Ofishal Puns

Cynthia MacGregor of New York accepts the blame for most of these.

Who's the famous fish with the pointing arm on the recruiting poster?
    Uncle Salmon.

Why did the fish get turned down by the Army?
    He failed his herring test.

How did the escargot cross the lake?
    By snail boat.

Why did the crustacean divorce her husband?
    He was an old crab.

How do you keep fish in jail?
    With strong lox.

Ten fishermen had a great day's catch at a small lake. Who was the saddest fish that evening?
    The sole survivor.

Who is the fish that always overeats?
Porgy pig.

How did the fish pay for expensive surgery?
He got a break on the price because he had a cousin who was a famous sturgeon.

What did the fisherman say to the magician? Take a cod, any cod.

How does Mama Salmon differentiate among her offspring?
She arranges them roe by row.

Why did the fish who was in a hurry hop on the back of another fish?
He knew he could travel faster on the pike.

Why didn't the fish want to make love?
He had a haddock.

What do fish sing on Sunday morning?
Nearer, my cod, to thee.

Why did the parakeet fly onto the fish's back?
He was looking for a perch.

Who defends the ocean from foreign invaders?
Sole-diers, snailors, and pilot fish.

Why did the minister spend so much time underwater?
He was interested in saving soles.

Ab and Eb were brothers. One day Momma fish got angry and yelled at Eb. Why?
Because Eb was a mean tease and he wouldn't leave Abalone.

What's the number-one song underwater?
"O Sole Mio."

Ms. MacGregor does not restrict her work to fish, as she sheepishly admits.

How does a sheep protect his driver's license?
    He has it lamb-inated.

What's the sheep's favorite comic strip?
    Mutton Jeff.

Where do sheep go when they want to barter?
    To the five-and-ten because they know they'll get their Wool-worth.

What do you read at a sheep funeral?
    A lamb-ment.

Why were the Platters the sheep's favorite singing group?
    Because one of their hits was "Only Ewe."

What football team did the ewe cheer for?
    No, not the rams! Navy, because she heard they kept everything sheep-shape.

An Answer to the Question: "How Far Can You Run with a Pun?"

Most people have heard this age-old question and answer:

What happened in the race between the lettuce, the faucet, and the tomato?
    Lettuce was head, faucet kept running, and tomato strained to ketchup.

Paul Zaslaw of Milton, Massachusetts, became concerned with the other participants in that race and posted these results:

GLUE ....was fast paste
EGG .... got cracking and scrambled away
MUG OF BEER ....was only a chaser
KANGAROO .... ran out of bounce
FLY .... lost its zip
ODOMETER .... was on the dash
STUDENT .... was unable to make a high grade in the course
BANANA .... peeled off fruitlessly
WATCH .... wound down and eventually stopped running
TOILET PAPER .... wiped out early
AUTHOR .... was Swift
DECK OF CARDS ....shuffled through
CHOCOLATE MILK .... was Quick, but took an early spill
SHRUB .... was a little bushed
SHOE .... really stepped on it
PROSTITUTE .... hustled through her opening lap
WHEEL ....lost its bearings
INK .... ran all over the place
JUNKIE .... was caught speeding
CREDIT CARD .... charged on
MANURE .... covered a lot of ground
TELEPHONE .... got hung up somewhere along the line
KNIFE .... just couldn't cut it
CALENDAR .... was observed only to March fourth
TAILOR .... let out long pants and pressed on
CENTAUR .... ran a half-assed race
STAIRCASE .... took a flight
FOREIGNER .... was Russian
PEN .... started skipping
KING'S CHAIR .... was thrown, of course
SPERM CELL .... petered out
PIPE .... tried running with clogs, but was soon drained
SOAP DISH .... was full of Zest
FROG .... croaked along the way

BULLDOZER ....tore up the road
NOSE ....never stopped running
BICYCLE .... was two-tired for racing
CHECK .... bounced on a loan
GROCER .... ran out of juice
DINNER JACKET ....was worn out
PENCIL .... was used to erase and lead to a point
NUT ....turned and bolted
CANDLE .... had a wicked start, but finally burned itself out
INVALID .... passed on toward the end
WAVES .... were not able to remain a wake
PLAYBOY .... got behind early
RABBIT .... hopped to it
TROUSERS .... slacked off, but ran a fine overall race
WOOL .... was on the lamb
VEGETABLE ....was beet
LITTLE MISS MUFFET ....lost her whey
DRESS .... was just a long jumper
PAINT ....started streaking

The Case of the Five-Hundred-Pound Canary

Martin S. Kottmeyer of Illinois wrote most of these ten years ago and claims he didn't want them unleashed on the world in these troubled times, but I convinced him that the world would be a better place if he let them out. To set the mood for this, Kottmeyer sent along a news clipping with the following lead paragraph:

500-POUND SPARROW ON LOOSE?
   Casper, Wyo. (UPI)—A deputy investigating the theft of 11 pounds of worms hopes a reward offered in the case won't produce any more tips like the one suggesting he question the nearest 500-pound sparrow.

What has four feet, four wings, four eyes, is yellow, and weighs half a ton?

Two five-hundred-pound canaries.

Why do five-hundred-pound canaries have wings?

So you can't tell them from duckbill platypuses.

Why are five-hundred-pound canaries rare?

Because a lot of people don't like them well-done.

Why are five-hundred-pound canaries tough?

Because they are so rare.

What should you look for when buying a five-hundred-pound canary?

The Good Housekeeping Seal of Approval.

What should you look for when buying several five-hundred-pound canaries?

A psychiatrist.

Group insurance.

How do you lure a five-hundred-pound canary to a trap?
Hide in the bushes and make a sound like birdseed.

Why do five-hundred-pound canaries wear yellow furry toe-warmers?
To keep their toes warm.
To lure yellow woolyworms for breakfast.

How do five-hundred-pound canaries get down chimneys?
Hide in Santa's toy sack, then wait until Christmas.

What happened to the five-hundred-pound canary that landed on the beach?
It became Sandy Claws.

If you push a six-thousand-year-old five-hundred-pound canary into a bowl of hot tomato soup, what happens?
It drowns—five-hundred-pound canaries can't swim.

What did the five-hundred-pound canary say while walking down the street?
Here, kitty, kitty, kitty.

How do you prevent five-hundred-pound canaries from charging?
Turn off their generators.

How do you prevent five-hundred-pound canaries from attacking you on safaris?
Use five-hundred-pound canary repellant.

What do five-hundred-pound canaries say when they are hungry?
CHIRP CHIRP.

Why do five-hundred-pound canaries have sharp beaks?
They make handy can openers.

Why don't five-hundred-pound canaries ride bicycles?
They have enough trouble trying to ride tricycles.

Why do five-hundred-pound canaries have feathers?
Because they'd look rather silly with fur on.

What weighs five-hundred pounds, is green, and smashes trees?
A five-hundred-pound tree frog.

What is big, lives near the beach, and wears sunglasses?
A hip five-hundred-pound seagull.

Why did the five-hundred-pound canary put its ear to the ground?
It wanted to know if a caterpillar stampede was headed its way.

Are five-hundred-pound canaries intelligent?
Of course not, they're all birdbrained.

What do five-hundred-pound canaries do on Halloween?
They go trick or tweeting.

What do five-hundred-pound canaries do on Thanksgiving?
They're glad they're not turkeys.

Why do five-hundred-pound canaries look fat?
They have poor dress designers.

When five-hundred-pound canaries fight caterpillars, who usually loses?
The five-hundred-pound canary usually ends up with de feet.

Why can't you trust five-hundred-pound canaries?
They're too cagey.

Why didn't the five-hundred-pound canary join the Air Force?
It didn't need an extra set of wings.

What's the difference between a five-hundred-pound canary and a regular canary?
Ex-Lax.

What do five-hundred-pound canaries do on Sundays?
 They go to chirp.

What is large, has never been photographed, and lives in Scotland?
 The Loch Ness canary.

What do you get if you cross a road with a five-hundred-pound canary?
 Run over.

If in a restaurant you must choose between eating an elephant egg or a five-hundred-pound canary egg, which should you choose?
 A five-hundred-pound canary egg, because everyone hates elephant yolks.

· 26 ·

Personal Worst

Several years ago, the Baltimore *Sun* published the 50 jokes that the National Association of Gagwriters had singled out as the oldest—and possibly worst—jokes of all time. Included were such classics as:

"Call me a taxi."
"Okay, you're a taxi."

and:

"I just flew in from California, and my arms are tired."

The NAG list underscores the point that some jokes are so bad that they are actually bad. Worse yet, here are some that are so bad they actually start to sound good.

Who is the first Irishman you see in the spring?

Patty O'Furniture.

Fighter: "I really want a shot at the Kid—Kid Jackson. I know I'm getting old and a little punchy, but before I retire I just want one chance in the ring with him."

Manager: "Look, if I've told you once, I've told you a hundred times. *You're* Kid Jackson."

Young woman to old man who has just asked her to marry: "What about sex?"

Old man: "Infrequently."

Young woman: "One word or two?"

Secretary: "Our files are so crowded that I suggest we destroy all correspondence more than six years old."

Boss: "By all means, but be sure to make copies first."

An uncle advised his nephew, "If you can make love to a woman as long as it takes to cook a chicken, you'll be a man."

Today the nephew owns a microwave oven.

"I'm so depressed, I had to shoot my dog."

"Was he mad?"

"He wasn't exactly pleased."

I had my nose broken in three places—Chicago, Philadelphia, and Baltimore.

An 89-year-old man and an 87-year-old woman go to an attorney's office asking for a divorce.

"This is crazy," says the lawyer. "You two have been married for over 60 years and you are getting a divorce now?"

"Look," says the husband, "we've been at each other's throat for decades now."

"Why did you wait so long?" the lawyer asks.

"Well," says the wife, "we just wanted to wait until the children were dead."

"Dad, there was a man here to see you today."

"Did he have a bill?"

"No, just an ordinary nose like yours."

Postman: "Is this package yours? The name is illegible."

Smith: "Can't be mine; my name is Smith."

"I really loved my vacation in California," said the lady on the plane to the man sitting next to her.

"Where did you stay?" he asked.

"San Jose."

"Madam, in California we pronounce the *J* as *H*. We say San Hosay. How long were you there?"

"All of Hune and most of Huly."

"Did you hear about the fire at the shoe factory?"

"No, what happened?"

"One hundred and fifty souls were lost."

Serious young man: "Do you enjoy Kipling?"

Young woman: "I don't know—how do you kipple?"

"I was shot in the leg in the war."

"Have a scar?"

"No, thanks, I don't smoke."

First woman: "Why, look who's coming up the street—my husband and my boyfriend."

Second woman: "Funny, I was about to say the same thing."

A man in his sixties is being sentenced to 30 years in the pen for robbing a bank at gunpoint.

"But judge," he pleads, "I may not be able to live out my sentence."

"Don't worry," replies the judge. "Just do what you can."

"Madam, in all my years in dentistry that's the biggest cavity I've ever seen. That's the biggest cavity I've ever seen."

"I heard you, doctor. You don't have to repeat yourself."

"Who's repeating?" says the dentist. "That was an echo."

An angry worker goes into her company's payroll office to complain that her paycheck is $50 short.

The payroll supervisor checks the books and says, "I see here that last week you were overpaid by $50. I can't recall your complaining about that."

"Well, I'm willing to overlook an occasional error, but this is two in a row."

A man is lost in the desert and is becoming increasingly thirsty. He meets a man on a donkey and asks if he can buy some water.

"No, but I will sell you my necktie for $10."

The man on foot replies, "No thanks, I don't need a tie. I need water."

"OK! Five bucks!" says the man on the donkey.

"No. I need water."

"OK! Two bucks and that's my final offer."

The man on foot walks away without saying another word.

Many hours later, he is crawling across the desert and spots a lush green oasis. He crawls to a man in a tux who has one hand on a velvet rope.

"Please! Is there any water?"

"Plenty," says the man in the tux, "inside."

"Please . . . please, let me in."

"I'm sorry, sir, but we require all gentlemen to wear ties."

Two elderly women sitting on a porch.

"Did you and your husband ever have mutual orgasm?"

"No, I think we had State Farm."

A drunk walks out of the Ritz Hotel, flops into a cab, and says, "Take me to the Ritz Hotel."

"We're there, sir."

"Okay," he says, throwing the driver a five-dollar bill, "but next time don't drive so fast."

A genie visits an elderly widow who sits with a tomcat at her feet. The genie offers her three wishes.

Disbelieving, she asks for a chest of gold. The gold appears.

Then she asks to be made into a young and beautiful woman, and she is.

Finally, she asks that her tired old tomcat be turned into a handsome young prince, and he is so transformed.

As the genie fades away, the last thing he hears is the prince saying to the beautiful young woman, "Now, aren't you sorry you had me neutered?"

Q. Where do you get your hair cut?
A. On the ends.

Q. Where is baseball mentioned in the Bible?
A. In the big inning.

Q. Who had the first computers in the Bible?
A. Adam and Eve—she had an Apple and he had the first Wang.

Q. Why is it useless to send a message to Washington?
A. Because he's dead.

Q. How do you catch a unique rabbit?
A. Unique up on it.

Q. How do you catch a tame rabbit?
A. Tame way, unique up on it.

Q. What does a dog do that a man steps in?
A. Pants.

Q. What is it that a cow has four of and a woman has two of?
A. Feet.

Q. What's green and sings?
A. Elvis Parsley.

Q. How can you have a Worst Joke list without at least ten Good News . . . Bad News Jokes?
A. Okay, you win—but only ten.

1. A baseball fanatic is visited by the ghost of an old teammate during the night. "Sam," says the ghost, "I've got good news—they play baseball in heaven."
"Thank God," says Sam.
"And the bad news is that they've got you starting tomorrow."

2. Galley chief to oarsman: "The good news is that you get a double ration of chow . . . the bad news is that the boss wants to go water-skiing after lunch."

3. Cardinal Bernardin called all of the priests of the Chicago archdiocese to the cathedral. He said, "I've got some good news and some bad news for you. First the good news: I've talked with God and everything is okay. Now the bad news: She called from Salt Lake City."

4. Moses, coming down from the mountain with stone tablets under his arm, is greeted by an anxious multitude. "Well, friends," he says, "I have good news and bad news. I'll give you the good news first: I've got him down to ten. Now the bad news: Adultery is still one of them."

5. The doctor calls with the results of Sam's physical.

"Sam I've got bad news and worse news. The bad news is that you have only 24 hours to live."

"Oh, no," says Sam. "That's rotten, but what could be worse that that?"

"I've been trying to get you since yesterday."

6. A man wakes up in the hopital after having his gangrenous leg amputated.

"How am I doing?" he asks the doctor.

"Well, I've got good news and bad news. The bad news is that we amputated the wrong leg.

"I don't believe what you're saying. What could possibly be the good news?"

"I think we're going to be able to save the other leg."

7. The good news is that I spotted the first robin of spring. The bad news is that he spotted me first.

8. Bad news: Your husband just ran off with your best friend.

Good news: That's two people off your Christmas list.

9. Bad news: Your wife just ran off with the gardener.

Good news: It's his day off.

10. Good news: Paramount and Columbia love your script treatment and, in fact, fought over it.

Bad news: Paramount and Columbia are the names of my dogs.

Patient (waking up after an operation): "Why are all the shades drawn?"
Doctor: "Well, there's a fire across the street, and I didn't want you to think the operation was a failure."

A couple in their late seventies went to the doctor's office. The doctor asked, "What can I do for you?" The man said, "Will you watch us have sexual intercourse?" The doctor looked puzzled, but agreed. When the couple had finished, the doctor said, "There is nothing wrong with the way you have intercourse." And he charged them $10. This happened several weeks in a row. The couple would make an appointment, have intercourse, pay the doctor, and leave. Finally the doctor said, "Just exactly what are you trying to find out?" The old man said, "We're not trying to find out anything. She is married, and we can't go to her house. I am married, and we can't go to my house. Holiday Inn charges $22 dollars; Hilton Hotel charges $27 dollars. We do it here for $10 and I get $8 back from Medicare for a visit to the doctor's office."

Why shouldn't the number 288 ever be mentioned in mixed company?
   Because it's two gross.

Sam: "Call me a cab, will you?"
Joe (in uniform): "I'm not the doorman; I'm a naval officer."
Sam: "Then call me a boat."

He: "A man picked my pocket."
She: "What did he get?"
He: "Practice."

Drunk: "Taxi?"
Driver: "Yes, sir!"
Drunk: "I thought so."

What do they call an abortion in Czechoslovakia?
   A canceled Czech.

What would you have if your canary got caught in your lawn mower?
   Shredded Tweet!

What did Cleopatra say when Mark Antony asked if she was true to him?

Omar Khayyam.

What do you call a legless bull?

Ground beef.

What do you call a boomerang that doesn't come back?

A stick.

Then there was the illegitimate Rice Krispie—snap, crackle, but no pop.

"Didn't you hear me pounding on the floor last night?"

"Oh, that's all right," replied the downstairs neighbor, "we were making a lot of noise ourselves."

A Southern woman ran up the path to the church and hurriedly asked a man, "Is Mass out?"

"No," said the man, "but your hat's on crooked."

A drunk is sitting at a bar next to a man and his wife. Suddenly he emits a tremendous belch.

"How dare you? What do you mean, belching before my wife?" demanded the man.

"Pardon me," says the drunk as he gets down off the stool, "I had no idea it was the lady's turn."

One cockroach runs into another in a drain.

"Did you hear about the new restaurant?" says one roach. "It's unbelievable—the refrigerator looks like polished silver, the shelves are clean as a whistle and—"

"Stop," says the other roach. "Not while I'm eating!"

Student: "Is this ice cream pure?"

Soda jerk: "As pure as the girl of your dreams."

Student: "Gimme a pack of cigarettes."

A man is registering at a hotel with a woman who is not his wife. He takes the pen handed to him by the room clerk and draws an X on the register. Then with a thoughtful look on his face, he circles the X.

"Lots of people sign with an X," says the clerk, "but this is the first time I've ever seen one with a circle around it."

"Nothing odd," says the man. "There are times when a person doesn't want to use his real name."

A man comes into a bar for the 26th night in a row, and the bartender asks him, "Jim, how come you never come in with a date?"

"Well," says Jim, "I work for the circus cleaning up the cages of the animals, and I stink so bad that I can't get close enough to a woman to ask her out."

"I noticed the horrible smell the first night you came through the door," said the bartender. "Why don't you quit this horrid job and go to work in an office?"

"What! And leave show business?"

Holdup man: "Stick 'em up or else."
Victim: "Or else what?"
Holdup man: "Don't confuse me—this is my first job."

Teacher: "Where was the Declaration of Independence signed?"
Kid: "At the bottom."

He: "Would you commit adultery for a million dollars?"
She: "Why, I think I might."
He: "How about two dollars?"
She: "What do you think I am?"
He: "We've settled that. What we're haggling about is the price."

Drugstore clerk: "Did you kill any moths with those mothballs I sold you the other day?"
Customer: "No, I tried for hours and couldn't hit one."

"I know a girl who can play the piano by ear."
"That's nothing. I know a man who fiddles with his whiskers."

"I'd like a pair of stockings for my wife."
"Sheer?"
"No, she's at home."

"What is nitrate of sodium?"
"I'd imagine it's half the day rate."

Two psychiatrists run into each other on the street. The first to speak says, "You're fine. How'm I doing?"

Watching his new employee count out the day's receipts, the boss walks over and asks the man where he got his financial training.
"Yale," he answers.
"Good. And what is your name?"
"Yackson."

Did you hear about the man whose cat got run over by a steamroller?
He didn't say anything—he just stood there with a long puss.

A man and woman met and married through a personal ad in the paper. Now there's a problem: Every time he picks the paper off the porch, she thinks he's cheating on her.

A man walks into a psychiatrist's office with a large hatbox. He opens it to reveal, to the doctor's shock, the head of a woman who is wearing a large flowered hat.
"This is terrible," the doctor gasps.
"Yeah," says the maniac, "that's what I told her when she paid $50 for it."

What's green and red and goes a hundred miles an hour?
    A frog in a blender.

"No," said the centipede, crossing her legs, "a hundred times no!"

"Send somebody over right away," said the excited lady on the phone to the policeman. "There's an enormous gray animal in my garden pulling up cabbages with his tail."
    "What's he doing?"
    "If I told you," said the woman, "you'd never believe me."

If two's company, and three's a crowd, what are four and five?
    Nine.

What's a metaphor?
    To keep cows in.

Why do bees hum?
    Because they don't know the lyrics.

All the animals came on the ark in pairs—except for the worms. They came in apples.

To whom it may concern:
    Please send me a copy of your most recent catalog and price list.
                        Most cordially,

    P.S. You need not send the catalog and price list. I have changed my mind.

"How do you feel after eating all those pancakes?"
    "Waffle."

*We interrupt these jokes to bring back three bop jokes from
the early 1950s.*

1. The man walking in front of the two bopsters falls into an open
manhole.

"Hey, fellows, give me a hand," he calls from underground.

"Okay," they say as they begin to applaud.

2. Two cats are finishing their meal. One says, "Think I'll have a
piece of apple pie."

"Sorry," says the waitress, "but the apple pie is gone."

"Crazy, I'll take two pieces."

3. "Man, dig that ocean," said the first bopster on seeing the
Pacific.

"That's nothin', pops," said the second. "That's only the top."

"I'm a pauper."

"Congratulations. Boy or girl?"

I'm on a seafood diet.

Every time I see food I eat it.

The answer is: Chicken Teriyaki.

The question is: Who is the world's only surviving kamikaze
pilot?

Confucius say:

"Many men smoke, but Fu Manchu."

"Wash face in morning. Neck at night."

"Husband who know where wife keep nickels has nothing
on one who know where maid's quarters are."

Why do the bees buzz?

You'd buzz, too, if someone stole your honey and nectar.

First fly: "Hey your human is open."
Second fly: "What?"
First fly: "April Fool!"

She: "I'm perfect."
He: "I'm practice."

Q. Why are birds melancholy in the morning?
 A. Because their little bills are all over dew.

"Papa, what's a vacuum?"
 "A vacuum is a void."
"I know, Papa, but vat's the void mean?"

"Answer the door."
 "Hello, door."

"Say good-night, Gracie."
 "Good-night, Gracie."

"You look like Helen Green."
 "I look worse in pink."

"How did I get here?" the little whisk broom demanded.
 His parents replied, "We swept together."

"I would like some alligator shoes."
 "What size shoes does your alligator wear?"

Did you hear about the cowardly dragon who only preyed on weak knights?

Then there was the chiropodist who was walking down the street and ran into one of his patients. At first he didn't recognize her, but when she spoke he said, "Oh, hello, there—I didn't know you with your shoes on."

· 27 ·

You Know You're Hearing a Joke When . . .

Thetebarometric bits of advice were a formula that came into its own in the 1980s when we needed all the help we could find in getting our bearings.

You Know You're Getting Older When . . .

. . . there's too much room in the house and not enough in the medicine cabinet.

. . . all the names in your little black book end in M.D.

. . . your back goes out more often than you do.

. . . your chidren begin to look middle aged.

. . . your grandchildren study things in history that you studied in current events.

. . . you renew your subscription to *Playboy*, but can't remember why (from Bob Orben).

. . . you call in sick and mean it.

. . . you can't tell one automobile from another.

. . . you turn out the bedroom light for economic reasons.

. . . your friends tells you that your stockings are badly wrinkled and sagging and you aren't wearing any.

. . . your knees buckle but your belt won't.

. . . your birthday cake collapses from the weight of the candles.

. . . you realize that the gleam in your eye is the sun reflecting on the bifocals.

. . . you can't get a rocking chair started.

. . . your mind makes contracts your body can't fulfill.

. . . you can only get rid of the wrinkles you see in the mirror by taking off your glasses.

. . . you look at the menu before eyeing the waitress (waiter).

. . . you look forward to a dull evening at home.

. . . you reach the top of the ladder and realize it was leaning against the wrong wall.

. . . you don't think this story is funny:
An old man is talking with his friends and reports, "I've got my health, everthing is fine, my heart and liver are great and my mind, knock wood . . . who's there?"

You Know It's Going to Be a Bad Day When . . .

. . . your mother calls and asks you to pay attention because they'll only allow her one call.

. . . a large man with a black cigar and a diamond pinky ring greets you with a kiss when you step onto the porch for the morning paper.

. . . your broker calls and launches into a long monologue about how Americans put too much emphasis on making money.

. . . your boss asks you for a ride home, and you recall that there are at least a dozen empty beer cans rolling around on the front floor and the latest issues of *Sluts in Heat* and *Raunchy Interludes* are on the front seat.

. . . you take your blind date to see *Swan Lake,* and he/she can't resist the urge to heckle the dancers.

. . . the Army expresses interest in the weapons potential of the gases coming from your compost pit.

. . . your business partner gets an unlisted number and won't give it to you.

. . . you put your bra on backwards and find that it fits better.

YOU KNOW YOU'RE HEARING A JOKE WHEN . . .

. . . you back your car into the motorcycle of a man who has "born to raise hell" tattooed on his forehead. He watches it fall over.

. . . your youngest child is selected to be the National Head Lice poster child.

. . . you meet your new neighbors and find that they are in the fat-rendering business and plan to work at home.

. . . you look out your window, and three surveyors from the state highway department wave back at you from your new patio.

. . . you watch the orthodondist drool as he gets a first look at one of your children.

. . . you are informed that a crew from "60 Minutes" is in your outer office.

. . . your twin forgets your birthday.

. . . nothing that you do seems to work in getting the vultures off your front lawn.

. . . you get a call from someone at the local IRS office, and the caller says you are a great morale booster—that they were looking at your deductions and most of them still haven't stopped laughing.

. . . you come home to find your wife having a riotous time with an old Army buddy of yours and are forced to remind them that you were never in the Army.

. . . you get a long sympathetic glance from an old friend at a party and later find that he/she is serving on a grand jury.

. . . you wake up face down on the pavement.

. . . your unemployed roommate announces that he thinks there is good money to be made cleaning septic tanks.

. . . your parents come to watch you play in a game and wear bags over their heads.

. . . you catch a glimpse of the exterminator you've hired running away from your house and note that something has caused his hair to suddenly turn white.

You Know You Have Employee Relations Problems When . . .

(A variation first encountered in Michael Iapoce's *A Funny Thing Happened on the Way to the Boardroom*)

. . . you have to ask Personnel to hire a food taster.

. . . your employees pledge that they won't be the first to use tactical nukes.

. . . your employees start referring to the parking lot as the DMZ.

· 28 ·

How to Tell a Joke

Before you start wondering "What makes this guy such an authority on joke-telling?" I'd better flash a few credentials.

I own nearly 300 joke books (ask my wife, please), have neatly marked files of jokes (with titles like "Light Bulb Jokes" and "Fly in My Soup Jokes"), and have published under my own name two joke books and a book of puns including the volume you hold in your hand.

There's more. I even have a small private joke "museum" in which I have collected such oddities as triple puns, jokes that got politicians in deepest hot water, and topical and antique jokes. To digress for a moment, the museum contains such fine items as:

Fad Jokes. For instance, the 3-D movie craze of the 1950s left such gems as these: Hollywood is now working on a 3-D film that, if you don't go into the theater to see it, comes out to see you. . . . Man at 3-D movie: "Lady, would you please remove your hat; I can't see." Lady: "I'm sorry, sir, it's part of the movie.". . . The Pentagon has just completed a movie made in 9-D, that's 3-D in triplicate. . . . "Baby, you'd look great in 3-D," said the producer to the starlet. "Would it be in Technicolor?" she responded. "No," said the producer, "that's my hotel-room number."

Multiple Puns. It has been claimed that this is as perfect a triple pun as the language offers. A woman's three sons go to Texas to raise cattle, hogs, and sheep. After a while, they write to her and say that all is fine except that they have been unable to come up with a name for the ranch.

"NAME IT FOCUS," she telegraphed.

The boys were puzzled and cabled back for an explanation.

Her reply: "FOCUS—WHERE THE SUN'S RAYS MEET."

Show Me's. As in "Show me a careless owl and I'll show you a bird that doesn't give a hoot."

Or's. As in: Or, as the fly said as he walked up the mirror, "That's another way of looking at it"; Or, as Lady Godiva said at the end of her famous ride, "I am drawing near to my close"; Or, as the ram said as he plunged off the cliff, "I didn't see that ewe turn"; and, Or, as the scientist said just after he had cloned himself, "I'm beside myself with happiness."

Inanimate Object Jokes. Such as the one can of paint that says to the other can of paint, "Darling, I think I'm pigment."

Lost Punch Lines. This wing of the museum was opened with the discovery of an essay by Burges Johnson, which appeared in the *Atlantic Monthly* for July 1952, in which he listed a large number of punch lines to jokes that, to quote Johnson, ". . . are no longer repeated in full by intelligent people who know that all other intelligent people know them." Johnson, a comic genius who among other things helped Mark Twain edit his *Library of Humor* and edited *Judge*, the comic weekly, listed punch lines to jokes that this author will spend years trying to reunite with their bodies. A few from that list:

"My brother is bringing the pineapples."
"The horse blew first."
"For heaven's sake sing."
"It was bitten off."
"Parts of it were excellent."
"Oh hell, make it Monday."
"Gosh, how I dread it."

Enough showing off. This is the important joke from the museum:

A mosquito lands on the ear of an elephant and says, "Mind if I grab a ride?"

"Not at all," replies the elephant. "I didn't notice you land and I won't notice you taking off."

This is not exactly a thigh-slapper, but it is a true museum piece because it was translated from a Babylonian tablet of the seventh century B.C. One of the reasons I love it is because it underscores the universality of talking-animal jokes. It allows one to imagine ancient Babylonians loving twentieth-century jokes that begin with set-ups like, "A poodle goes into a bar and orders a martini . . ."

More proof? In 1986 I became a celebrity for about 15 minutes when I wrote a short impassioned plea for recognition of the 50th anniversary of the knock-knock joke in a local magazine, and more than 50 newspapers and the *Reader's Digest* chose to reprint it. Come to think of it, I may have been the only person in America upset by the fact that there wasn't a commemorative stamp or a Congressionally mandated National Knock-Knock Week. Moreover, I may have been the only person in America who knew and took seriously the fact that it was the 50th anniversary of the knock-knock joke fad, which had been, as previously reported in this book, invented by Dorothy Parker for the Algonquin Round Table in the 1920s and took the country by storm in 1936.

I say all of this not to show off, but to underscore the fact that I am serious about jokes and that my joke credentials are in order. Yet, as much as I love jokes and continue to collect and dote on them, I am still a semi-marginal OK joke teller who only occasionally hits home with the right joke told in the right manner at the right time. I am good enough to know that there are few feelings quite as spectacular as when you string a few hundred words together and reduce a cluster of erect and sober fellow human beings to a goofy ring of bent-over, watery eyed, wheezing thigh-slappers. This is power.

On the other hand, I know how it feels to fail—to suddenly realize that the joke coming out of your mouth is bombing and that even the perfect punch line is not going to save you. It is the feeling that actors on the opening night of a bad play call "flop sweat." One learns quite quickly that reading a joke is a far cry from telling a joke and vice-versa. Speaker and joke writer Bob Orben, whose many clients have ranged from Red Skelton to Gerald Ford to the heads of major corporations, is fond of pointing out that the routine "Who's On First?" does not look funny on paper but was dynamite when performed by Abbott and Costello.

The question raised here is this: Can joke telling be reduced to a series of rules and ruminations that will make one a better joke teller?

Perhaps not. If you lack the timing, determination, and basic aptitude you do not stand a chance. It has been said that if you are a person who says things like "I'm really no good at telling stories—I can't even remember them" you should not even try. It is the equivalent of saying, "I'm really no good at driving—I can never remember which is the road and which is the sidewalk." If you tell jokes to only underscore a point of view—liberalism/conservatism, pro-this/anti-that —you are predestined to be as witty as the *Congressional Record.*

Moreover, jokes specifically and humor in general seem to resist formal analysis. "We must understand that all sentences which begin with *W* are funny," is what Robert Benchley, once said in making fun of those looking for tips on how to be funny.

However, the idea of a basic course in joke telling is appealing because even those who simply lack the ability should enjoy a tutorial on joke dynamics (just as thousands read Ted Williams's *Science of Hitting* who would be hard pressed to lay down a feeble bunt at the company picnic softball game).

Here then is a set of basic rules compiled with the help of others starting with author, linguist, and humorist Leo Rosten who long ago established himself as one of the reigning experts on how to tell a joke.

Control and manipulate.

Leo Rosten says that the key to telling jokes is the ability to read and master the situation at hand. "An audience, even one or two people, must be approached with confidence and no uncertainty or weakness." "Audiences," he says "do not give themselves to poor manipulators. For instance, you do not want to create an initial resistance to the joke so you don't want to start with a promise or an apology."

The kind of prefatory lines that invite resistance and drive Rosten crazy range from "This will really put you on the floor laughing—the funniest joke you've ever heard" to "I'm not sure I can tell this one right or even if it is that funny to begin with, but here goes." Master joke writer Bob Orben says that "prefacing" is even more of a liability when telling a joke in front of a large audience. "The only thing worse than saying 'that reminds me of a joke'," says Orben, "is saying 'that reminds me of an old joke.' You're telling the audience you didn't even bother to find a current joke."

Develop a technique. Borrow if you have to.

There are certain techniques that help get you from the set-up line to the climax or punch line. Your goal is rapt attention. Those who are the best joke tellers are those who use various physical and verbal devices to tell their stories and cue the laughter. These devices include smiles and chuckles, significant pauses and gasps of astonishment, exaggerated hand gestures and body English—almost anything that would be used by an actor.

You can learn this technique by studying the greats. Leo Rosten says that if you really want to get good at it, you should tape and study the televised appearances of the best comedians. "You don't do this to learn the jokes, but to learn the techniques. You watch where and when they pause in the telling of a story, how they use a quick chuckle or other mannerism to signal the audience that the punch line is coming." He adds, "Also watch their response to big laughs, small laughs, and jokes that don't work."

Rosten, who has seen all of the masters work, thinks that three of the best technicians working today are David Steinberg, Billy

Crystal, and Jay Leno. Bob Hope works from a script and some of the jokes in that script are not that funny, but Rosten points out that they become funny because of Hope's "impudence"— the style in which they are presented—and the mastery he imposes on his audience.

Rosten says that such study will reveal a lot about what works and what does not. For instance, he points out that great joke tellers tend to use simple verbs (complex verbs take one's attention away from the story), stay clear of introducing extraneous characters into their stories, and only use dialect when they are masters of it. "It is remarkable to me how many jokes are ruined by a bad accent or dialect" he says, pointing out that most professional comics know this and stay away from them.

Know your punch line.

William Novak, who is best known for his collaborative writing efforts with Lee Iacocca (*Iacocca*), Thomas "Tip" O'Neill (*Man of the House*), and Nancy Reagan (*My Turn*), is a student of humor, a joke collector, and co-author of *The Big Book of Jewish Humor* and *The Big Book of American Humor*. Novak is concerned with punch lines and their abuse. He believes that there should be absolutely no uncertainty or floundering in delivering the punch line. "This should not be left to chance. If you're going to tell a joke make sure you've worked out the rhythm and exact language of the punch line. Do what you have to do to make it work. Practice. If the punch line is a line called out from a distance, cup your hands around your mouth to give the illusion that you are yelling."

"Above all," says Novak in the matter of punch lines, "don't give it away in advance. Don't, for example, ask if they've heard a joke about the ... whatever ... and give away the joke in the process." Novak says that he knows this is an obvious point, but that it has to be made because it amazes him how often he hears people inadvertently kill good jokes.

Bob Orben has important advice on the punch line that is especially appropriate when telling jokes to large audiences. "Telling a joke in public is a frightening thing. You are on the line looking out at people and asking them to react to what you have to say. Because of this people will often deliver the punch line and go right past it without pausing. There is a split second—which can seem like an eternity—that has to be kept open for the audience's reaction. If you don't allow for that moment you'll be stepping on your own lines."

If you can handle it, embellish and customize.

"There is an old joke telling rule which says that if you lack skill as a joke teller that you should keep your jokes as simple and direct as possible," says Moshe Waldoks, co-author with William Novak on the Jewish and American humor books. "I agree with this, but I also think that if you are any good at it you should tell a story and do all sorts of things to make it a good story. I give as many as 75 speeches a year on humor and in them I tell jokes. What I'm saying to my audience is that you are going along for a ride. Enjoy it with me." Waldoks draws out his best stories, and it will take him 20 or 30 minutes to tell five or six jokes working in gags, details, and illusions along the way.

Frank Getlein, a Washington writer and art critic, is also known for his ability to tell a good joke or story, and his advice is similar but, if anything, goes further. "Learn to know when you have control of your audience and then learn to hold them with embellishment and detail. If you have created a mood of expectation and are in complete control, don't be afraid to stretch it out, to hold onto it. If everything is working, don't be afraid to turn it into a real production."

Flirt with the truth. Get real.

Bob Orben is a great believer in how you frame your jokes. "Framing doesn't really matter if you are telling a quick joke to someone you run into on the street, but it becomes very important with any kind of audience. And the best frame of all is the truth—the illusion that the joke is based on first-hand knowledge or experience."

He says this is what was happening when the old time vaudevillian would come onstage and look around furtively as if he was being chased. Then in a loud stage whisper—so as not to be "overheard"—he would begin with a line like, "You'll never believe what just happened to me." Old, but as Orben puts it, "a good frame."

Moshe Waldoks believes that you should customize jokes with an eye on the audience. "I don't tell jokes about a someone walking down Main Street. If I'm in Los Angeles I tell about someone walking down Wilshire Boulevard and if I'm in Boston it's Boyleston Street."

Listening to Waldoks tell a joke, one can hear him put his rules into play. For instance, he shies away from generic phrases like "this woman," "a football team," or "an airport." He assumes that we do not care about "this doctor" but do care about "a world-famous cardiologist."

The most successful humor is often self-deprecating. In other words, if you're going to make fun of someone start with yourself.

"I've been accused of being a dull speaker," said Senator John Glenn some years back adding, "Boring maybe, dull never." The senator has been widely and warmly quoted for that line for good reason. As a legitimate space hero and a member of the U.S. Senate, Glenn is an admired and powerful man. The joke is funny and memorable because in a few well-chosen words he is telling us that he is neither arrogant nor does he take himself too seriously. Ronald Reagan's best presidential lines—the ones that are already showing up in collections of great quotations—are those that underscore his fallibility: "You know by the time you reach my age, you've made plenty of mistakes if you've lived your life properly."

President Reagan was an expert teller of jokes but slipped on one or two occasions, such as the moment in 1985, when he quipped in regard to the Soviet grain deal that America "should keep the grain and export the farmers." This did not play well, especially since he had just vetoed farm credit legislation, and the nation was in the midst of a farm crisis.

The lesson for those of us not on the higher rungs of political power is that the joke that is a barb or jab is likely to bomb if it is aimed at others, especially if they are less powerful. Judith "Miss Manners" Martin takes its one step further. In her *Guide to Excruciatingly Correct Behavior*, she gives guidelines for joke telling and ends with this one: "The only truly safe and proper subject for a joke is oneself. Many a person who thought this privilege extended to his or her spouse, parent, or child, has lived—but not very long—to find otherwise."

When in doubt, don't tell it.

Many jokes rely on pain, predisposition, and pathos. "The secret source of humor itself is not joy," Mark Twain once wrote, "but sorrow. There is no humor in heaven." One can argue Twain's point (much humor and almost all puns are based on nothing more than word play), but recognize the pain in some jokes.

One must err on the side of conservatism in this regard. If there is the slightest nagging suspicion in your mind that the joke you are about to utter is going to make someone uncomfortable, obey your instincts. Bury the joke, forgo the laugh. As British publisher and politician Brendan Bracken put it many years ago, "It's a good deed to forget a poor joke."

One cannot be too careful in matters of race and religion, especially in jokes that involve slurs. Almost everyone who offered advice for this chapter said that if you are going to tell an ethnic, racial, or religious joke, that it had better be about the group that the joke teller belongs to—in other words, priests can get away with jokes about priests, and rabbis can tell rabbi jokes. Orben, who wrote for Dick Gregory for seven years, is quick to point out that he wrote lines and jokes the black comic could use, but that he couldn't.

As this book was nearing completion, there was a flurry of dumb blonde jokes making the rounds. This collector was sent several single-spaced sheets of these reworkings of the old slur jokes (the least venal example: What did the blonde call her pet zebra? Spot) and considered for a brief, half-witted moment running a collection of them in the "worst jokes" section.

A few days after filing them away, I was sent a column by Diane White of the *Boston Globe*. Ms. White is a very funny person and may have written one of the funniest send-ups of 1991 in her column on trying to explain the Red Sox to one's children—in reaction to all the solemn articles on explaining Pee Wee Herman's embarrassing problems to children. White's reaction to these blonde jokes? She smiled at first, then as they got nasty ("not nasty as in dirty but nasty as in ugly"), she wished that she hadn't smiled and asked herself, "Why shouldn't you laugh at a joke that pokes fun at blondes?" Her answer, in part, as it appeared in the October 3, 1991, *Globe*: "Because if you substitute the word 'woman' for blonde, you get the real drift of these jokes. . . . Blonde jokes are another manifestation of what I think of as the new misogyny."

'Nuff said? And that goes for those who say, as a man in White's office put it, "But I got it from a blonde."

On the other hand, this does not mean that you cannot tell jokes that rely on group perceptions that have nothing to do with race, religion, or national origin. If, for instance, anyone living in the Washington D.C. area could not tell lawyer, lobbyist, and legislator jokes, his or her repertoire would be reduced to "Why did the chicken cross the road?" jokes.

The one-liner that is as much a part of Chicago as the Cubs is the observation that it was so cold last night that they found an alderman with his hands in his own pockets. Politicians are fair game, as are doctors, sex therapists, professors, psychiatrists, barbers, lawyers, macho men, generals, admirals, tourists, Californians, the wealthy, the middle class, indulgent parents, suburbanites, Yankees, mountain people, flatlanders, bankers, and insurance agents.

The point is that few of us like a bigot or a bully. Also off limits—besides the obvious racial and religious jokes—are stammerers, the senile, the homeless, and just about anyone else who lacks power in the context of the joke. Disease and disability? Colds, baldness, mild allergies, hernias, toothaches, bunions, boils, and pimples are funny. Almost everything else isn't. Period.

Death is a proper subject but only in the right context, for instance, the formula joke in which St. Peter greets the deceased at the pearly gates.

Bob Orben, who has acted as a humor consultant to many powerful people in politics and business, adds that one of the hardest points to convince people of is, as he puts it, "sexist ain't funny." He points out that some of the worst offenders are people who wouldn't think of telling a racist joke.

Remember kids, don't try this at home.

There was a time when what you heard in the movie theater or coming out of your television set was very tame, and there were lines that one crossed only at personal peril. In February 1960, a joke was cut from the Jack Paar "Tonight" show on NBC that caused a great deal of controversy and led to his on-camera resignation. The joke was a long, involved story that relied on the confusion over the term "W.C." for a water closet (what the British call a toilet) and "W.C." for Wayside Chapel. In the joke, a schoolmaster is describing the chapel and says, for example, to the lady looking for plumbing: "It may interest you to know that my daughter was married in the W.C., and it was there that she met her husband."

Today the W.C. story would'nt even be seen as risque, and the line that Paar crossed doesn't exist anymore. The R-rated movie comedy, nightly cable TV offerings, radio "shock-jocks," taboo-less comedy clubs, and the racier network sitcoms create new lines that are then routinely crossed and recrossed.

The point is that, while one can get away with aping some of this, what works for Richard Pryor in a Los Angeles comedy club is likely to work *against* one at a neighborhood barbecue (unless your neighborhood is Sunset Strip). Don't try to copy those who rely on shock and taboos. Somebody like Richard Pryor can get away with it, but one of the reasons he can is, as Leo Rosten puts it, because he has such a "strong persona."

Another point to recall is that people voluntarily seek out raw comedy clubs. They stand in lines, pay covers and miniums, and pay cable TV charges for it. They seek it when they are in the mood. In the context of a business meeting, dinner party, or any of a hundred other venues, such humor is all but guaranteed to bomb big. It is akin to putting Scotch whiskey on someone's breakfast cereal because that person will occasionally order a Scotch and water at a cocktail party.

This is not to say that a good joke teller should not occasionally risk the risque—as Mae West once put it, "It's hard to be funny when you have to be clean." But if you enter the blue zone, do it with words that you wouldn't be afraid to use in front of your sixth grade teacher. Orben puts it this way: "Sex and sexual relations are long-established legitimate subjects for joke telling, just realize that there a lot of people like me who are offended by bad language and sexism which is different than sex. Sex is funny."

· 29 ·

Joke Books and Magazines

*Wit and humor are the distinctive possession of all
mankind, and form a vital area of literature that
deserves recognition and preservation.*

—Nat Schmulowitz

It may rank low in the galaxy of modern outrages, but it is, in
my opinion, an outrage nonetheless; written humor in general, and jokes in particular, are held in low esteem by libraries.
Therefore, one of the problems that face joke collectors is that
joke books and joke magazines are damnably difficult to find. For
instance, the Library of Congress has but a pitiful handful of the
joke magazines and paperback originals that were so common in
America from the 1920s through the early 1960s—the Golden Age
of pulp joke offerings. One is likely to find a better selection of
these classics at a good flea market.

Periodicals with pep and spunk (and, of course, *laffs*) are about as common as Gutenberg Bibles at our major libraries, which often have never even heard of such offerings as *Fun House, Pepper, Broadway Laughs, Jackpot, Popular Jokes, Good Humor, Laff Parade, Zowie, Romp, Jest, Army Laughs, A Laugh a Minit, Cartoons and Gags, Riot,* and *Laffing Out Loud.* Most good collections of such material are in private hands.

The only bright light is the San Francisco Public Library, which houses the Schmulowitz Collection of Wit and Humor (SCOWAH). It was originally put together by the late Nat Schmulowitz, a prominent San Francisco attorney, and now contains more than 17,000 books and a huge collection of magazines and other materials. It is housed in a large, crammed room in the library, and to walk through it, as I have, is to see the phenomenal assortment of material that has been published. To the joke lover, it is the Louvre, the Prado, and the Sistine Chapel rolled into one. One's eyes and mind boggle to see two shelves of Joe Miller joke books (one dating back to 1743), piles of old college humor magazines, more Benchley than a person could carry, and funny stuff in Finnish, Chinese, Tshi, and Gujarati (among the titles in Gujarati: *Tunki Ane Tach Ramuljo* and, of course, *Pratham Drastive Prem*).

Schumlowitz started the collection in 1947, when he gave the library 93 books, and he spent a great deal of his spare time from then until his death in 1966 adding to the collection.* He should be an inspiration to others who believe that libraries should shelter a little more laughter.

For budding collectors, here are a few quick tips: (1) Grab up as many of the old magazines and early paperbacks as you can. For the present they are great fun. As for the future, someday

---

* If the name rings a bell, Schmulowitz was the successful defense attorney in one of the twentieth century's most celebrated murder trials. He defended comedian Roscoe "Fatty" Arbuckle in the 1920s.

the libraries will wake up and you will be able to donate them and take a $1.3 million tax deduction. (2) Don't ever pass up a copy of the old *1000 Jokes* magazine, which was published from the 1930s through 1966. Great stuff. (3) Also, don't buy that line about old jokes not being funny because of changing fashions and sensibilities. There were many joke books published after 1900 that are still very funny. There are, of course, duds, too, but even these are interesting because of the number of times you run into an ancient form of a joke which you were told in the last few weeks with the preface "I just heard a new one . . ."

· **30** ·

But Seriously, Folks . . .

Small groups of persons without a sense of humor can do as much damage to America as small groups of communists in high places.

—William F. Treadwell
before meeting the American Public
Relations Society, February 21, 1955.

I am deeply indebted to a number of people for their help collecting the jokes needed for this book. Together they make up the counterforce to those knots of humorless subversives capable of doing so much damage to the Republic.

Bob Ackley
Don Addis
Nancy Alden
Reinhold Aman

W. R. Anderson
Joseph E. Badger
Kent Bailey
Mike Baldwin

Karen Marie Bartol

David F. Berger

Charlie Boon

Caroline Bryan

Larry Bryant

Samuel Cabot

C. H. Channing

John Clark

William Cole

Glenn Collins

Maureen Connolly

Charles Conrad III

Paul W. Corchran, M.D.

Martha Cornog

Don Crinklaw

Clifford Crist

S. Percy Dean

John R. DeMonte

Al deQuoy

Arthur J. Deex

C. Henry Depew

Tom Dial

Nancy Dickson

Russell J. Dunn, Sr.

T. S. Durham

Frederick C. Dyer

Pat H. Everett

John D. Fitzgerald

Steve Fried

Joel Garreau

Walt Giachini

James G. Gillivan

Jeffrey H. Goldstein

Joel Goodman

Rev. Frederick G. Gotwald

Joseph C. Goulden

Fr. Don Graff

Marvin Grosswirth

Steven Haase

Irving Hale

Aronld Harris

N. Sally Hass

John M. Hazlitt

George A. Heinemann

Howard F. Heller, M.D.

William Heller

Archie Edward Hinson

Adrian W. Janes

Pat Jett

Geraldo Joffe

George Johnson

Janis Jones

Shel Kagan

Ron Kaye

Martin S. Kottmeyer

Norbert Kraich

Mary Kramer

Alan G. Lewis

David S. Little

Kenneth B. Livingston

Mel Loftus

Dale Lowdermilk

Neil Harding McAlister, M.D.

Cynthia MacGregor

Norman Mark

Steve Masse

Charles Mintzlaff

Paul Mouchon

Leslie Nelson
Bob Orben
Charles L. Orr
Dennis Panke
Herbert H. Paper
J. Beauregard Pepys
Timothy Perper
Irene H. Phillippe
Tom Quantance
Suzie Radus
Mark Rausch
Ross Reader
Harvey Roehl
William A. Rooney
Cornelius Van S. Roosevelt
Jim Rubins
William Safire
Jeffrey S. Sawtelle
Lauren Barnett Scharf
Penny Scott and her students
John Seiffer
Robert W. Sellen
Johnathan S. Silber
Bob Skole
Robert Smith
Richard C. Smolik

R. C. Snider
George R. Soika
John A. Staedler
Ashley Steele
Charles Stearns
Jeff Strickler
William Tammeus
Mike Thaler
John G. Thompson
Elizabeth Thorpe
James Thorpe III
Robert J. Throckmorton
Elaine Viets
William P. Wagner
Judie Wayman
Mike Weber
Rozanne Weissman
Robert T. West
Roy West
Craig Wheatley
Neal Wilgus
Ed Woodward
Sara Woodward
John C. Youngman, Sr.
Paul Zaslaw

Thanks again, or, as the woman said to her urologist husband, "Having you around makes a vas deferens."

Anyone who would like to suggest new ideas for the aforementioned joke museum or wants to contribute jokes can write to the author care of: Joke Museum, Box 80, Garrett Park, Maryland 20896.

Bibliography
(Sort of)

There is very few good judges of humor, and they don't agree.

—Josh Billings

In putting this collection together, I read or looked at hundreds of joke books ranging in quality from the outstanding to the dismal. Listed bibliographically with occasional notes are those that I liked best and could serve as guides to anyone building a collection. Of course, this is one man's opinion, and you may not agree.

Adams, Joey. *From Gags to Riches.* New York: Frederick Fell Inc., 1946.

Adams, Joey. *Joey Adams Joke Book.* New York: Frederick Fell Inc., 1952.

Adams, Joey. *Joey Adams Joke Dictionary*. New York: Citadel, 1962.

(All of these are treasure troves, especially the last one listed.)

Adler, Larry. *Jokes and How to Tell Them*. Garden City: Doubleday, 1963. (This unusual book really does tell you how to deliver a joke. The examples he uses are first-rate.)

Asimov, Isaac. *Treasury of Humor*. Boston: Houghton Mifflin Company, 1971. (Everyone interested in jokes should have this smashingly good collection.)

Blake, Robert. *101 Elephant Jokes*. New York: Pyramid Books, 1964. (You've got to have one of these, and this one is the best of the elephant lot.)

Boone, Charlie, and Roger Erickson. *The Worst of Boone and Erickson*. Minneapolis: WCCO Radio, 1977.

Cagney, Peter. *Treasury of Wit and Humor*. Preston: A. Thomas and Co., 1965.

Carlinsky, Dan. *A Century of College Humor*. New York: Random House, 1971.

Cerf, Bennett. (All of his joke collections, which number 15. All of them are good, although some jokes show up in more than one book. I can't imagine anyone interested in jokes not having a bunch of these books.)

Clark, David Allen. *Jokes, Puns and Riddles*. New York: Doubleday, 1968.

Coggins, Herbert L. *Knick Knacks*. Philadelphia: Penn Publishing Co., 1906.

Cohen, Myron. *The Myron Cohen Joke Book*. New York: Gramercy, 1978.

Copeland, Lewis. *The World's Best Jokes*. New York: Halcyon House, 1936.

Croy, Homer. *What Grandpa Laughed At*. New York: Duell, Sloan and Pearce, 1948.

David McKay Publisher. *A Thousand and One Riddles with a Few Thrown In*. Philadelphia: no date.

Davis, J. J. *The Entomologists' Jokebook.* Exterminator's Log. Lafayette, Ind., 1937.

Dickson, Paul, *Jokes.* New York: Delacorte, 1984. (Crude early version of this book—dates back to a simpler time when Elvis was still dead.)

Esar, Evan. *Esar's Comic Dictionary.* New York: Harvest House, 1943.

Esar, Evan. *The Humor of Humor.* New York: Bramhall House, 1952.

Fadiman, Clifton. *Any Number Can Play.* Cleveland: World, 1957. (Especially important for Fadiman's essay on punning.)

Fechtner, Leopold. *Encyclopedia of Ad-Libs, Insults and Wisecracks.* West Nyack, N.Y.: Parker Publishing Co., 1977.

Fechtner, Leopold. *5,000 One and Two Liners for Any and Every Occasion.* West Nyack, N.Y.: Parker Publishing Co., 1973.

Fredericks, Vic. *Crackers in Bed.* New York: Pocket Books, 1953.

Gigem Press. *The Best of 606 Aggie Jokes.* Dallas: 1976.

Golden, Francis Leo. *Laughter is Legal.* New York: Frederick Fell, 1950.

Hample, Stoo. *Silly Joke Book.* New York: Delacorte Press, 1978.

Hart, Harold. *Top Stuff.* New York: Parker Press, 1945.

Hershfield, Harry. *The Harry Hershfield Joke Book.* New York: Ballantine Books, 1964.

Hershfield, Harry. *Laugh Louder, Live Longer.* New York: Grayson Publishing Co., 1959.

Hershfield, Harry. *Now I'll Tell One.* New York: Greenberg, 1938.

Iapoce, Michael. *A Funny Thing Happened on the Way to the Boardroom.* New York: John Wiley & Sons, 1988.

Keller, Charles. *Laughing.* Englewoods Cliffs, N.J.: Prentice-Hall, Inc., 1977.

Keseling, Peter C., and John Kinney. *Summa Cum Laughter.* New York: Waldorf Publishing Corp., 1956.

Kopper, Richard, Richard Irvine, and John Burns. *A Treasury of College Humor.* New York: William Penn Publishing Co., 1950.

Lake, Anthony B. *A Pleasury of Witticisms and Word Play*. New York: Bramhall, 1965.

Lauber, Patricia. *Jokes and More Jokes*. New York: Scholastic Book Services, 1967.

Leeming, Joseph. *Riddles, Riddles, Riddles*. New York: Franklin Watts, Inc., 1953.

Levinson, Leonard. *Webster's Unafraid Dictionary*. New York: Macmillan, 1967.

Lieberman, Jerry. *Off the Cuff*. New York: Pocket Books, 1956.

McCarthy, Joe. *In One Ear*. New York: Doubleday, 1962.

Moger, Art. *The Complete Pun Book*. Secaucus, N.J.: Citadel Press, 1979.

Moulten, Powers. *2500 Jokes*. New York: New Home Library, 1942.

Murray, Ken. *Giant Joke Book*. New York: Ace Books, 1954.

Orben, Robert. (All of his titles. Orben is the king of one-line comedy, and he has lines for every subject under the sun. Especially recommended is *2100 Laughs for All Occasions*, Doubleday, 1982.)

Partridge, Eric. *The Shaggy Dog Story*. New York: Philosophical Library, 1954.

Pietsch, Jim. *The New York City Cab Driver's Joke Book*. New York: Warner Books, 1986. (Great premise—a real New York City cabbie asks real riders for their favorite jokes—with great mostly R-rated results.)

Price/Stern/Sloan publishers. *The Elephant Book*. Los Angeles: 1972.

Ripley, Elizabeth. *Lots of Laughs*. New York: Oxford University Press, 1942.

Rosten, Leo. *The Giant Book of Laughter*. New York: Crown, 1989.

Schwartz, Alvin. *Tomfoolery*. Philadelphia: J. B. Lippincott, 1973.

Shulman, Max. *Guided Tour of Campus Humor*. Garden City: Hanover House, 1955.

Smith, H. Allen. *Buskin' with H. Allen Smith*. New York: Pocket Books, 1969.

Tolliver, Bernard, P. *Barrel of Laughs.* New York: Hart Publishing Co., 1960.

Untermeyer, Louis. *A Treasury of Laughter.* New York: Simon and Schuster, 1946.

Wachs, Mark. *The Funniest Jokes and How to Tell Them.* New York: Hawthorne, 1968.

Wells, Carolyn. *Such Nonsense.* New York: George H. Doran Co., 1918.

Wilde, Larry. (All of his titles. Wilde is the most prolific of modern joke book writers, and each of his books covers a subject from A to Z. To date he has covered most of the major ethnic targets.)

Winick, Charles. *Outer Space Humor.* Mount Vernon, N.Y.: Peter Pauper Press, 1963.

Wright, Milton. *What's Funny and Why.* New York: Harvest House, 1953.

Yates, Bill. *Laughing on the Inside.* New York: Dell Publishing Co., 1953.

Youngman, Henny. (All of his titles. Take them all . . . please!)